SO YOU'RE GONNA RETIRE

HIT YOUR "NOW WHAT? BUTTON"
TALK, PLAN, "RE-TIRE". ENTER THE NEW RETIREMENT AGE

MARLENE M ROSENKOETTER, PHD, RN, FAAN

LifeRich Publishing is a registered trademark of The Reader's Digest Association, Inc.

LifeRich Publishing books may be ordered through booksellers or by contacting:

LifeRich Publishing
1663 Liberty Drive
Bloomington, IN 47403
www.liferichpublishing.com
1 (888) 238-8637

ISBN: 978-1-4897-0665-2 (sc)
ISBN: 978-1-4897-0666-9 (e)

Print information available on the last page.

LifeRich Publishing rev. date: 01/27/2016

DEDICATION

To The Many Retirees and Students Who Have Enriched My Life

ACKNOWLEDGMENTS

No book can be written in isolation, and this one is no exception. I gratefully acknowledge the assistance and wise counsel of those who have given so conscientiously of their time and offered assistance on the many topics in this book. Appreciation is expressed to Dr. Dixie Koldjeski for teaching about life pattern changes, to Dr. Debra Pierce and Dr. Cynthia Chernecky for their insights, and to the many others who provided comments.

DISCLAIMER

While the situations may reflect actual occurrences, the names used in this book do not represent the names of any actual people.

CONTENTS

PREFACE

This books is designed to assist people who are considering retirement to plan for both the transition and the experience. It presents ideas for those who are already retired and not adjusting well in order to make changes that will increase their satisfaction with being retired. The book provides strategies to improve communication as a fundamental technique in any dialogue with family and friends. Six major life patterns are discussed along with changes that can occur with retirement. A variety of assessment tools are presented that give the reader the opportunity to determine what to expect, and how to deal with the changes that can happen as a part of the retirement journey.

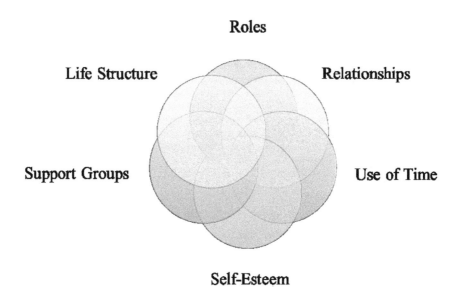

THE NEW RETIREMENT AGE

Life is like a coin. You can spend it any way you wish,
but you only spend it once. - Lillian Dickson

Basics of the Journey

Retirement used to mean you were *"over the hill"* – a sign you were getting old – or more importantly, that you were already there! But this has changed dramatically over the past two decades. More and more people are choosing *not* to retire, or to retire and then *unretire.* Many have decided to try out an entirely new career, a new job and enter *"worktirement"* as well as a new way of life. Over 70% of people thinking about retirement these days plan to work after they retire. There are now people in the work force who are in their 70's, 80's and even 90's. For them, the question is not *"Should I retire?"* or *"When should I retire?"* but rather, *"Why should I retire? I like working."*

When plans for your actual retirement become a reality, the most important question to ask yourself is, *"What am I going to do with myself after I do retire?"* Some folks don't retire until they are simply no longer able to do the work, or maybe they have totally lost interest in their jobs. Work has stopped being rewarding. Others just quit, and walk out. Some are forced to retire. People are retiring younger, in their 40s and 50s with several decades of productive and meaningful years ahead of them. They now have to plan for the rest of their lives, without their career or work to consume their time – also without a job that provides financial security and increases personal self-esteem. Others don't ever plan to fully retire and will continue working, full-time or part-time well after retirement age.

Indeed the entire retirement scene has changed, but what is clear is that *any* retirement – including *your* retirement – involves a major adjustment. One of the problems is that you have had little practice for the experience. Even taking a longer vacation, or going part-time, isn't really the same as totally quitting work. Retirement needs serious planning and preparation for the many changes that will occur. And you don't have to make *aging* the focus of your retirement. You can learn to enjoy the journey, the changes, and embrace the fact that many events in your new life will not always be predictable. But planning can help you cope with the experience. Retirement should be the *wisdom years*, and you can share that wisdom in many forms.

Retirement symbolizes the "wisdom years".
So share your wisdom.

Life after work sets you on a new journey – one of the greatest and potentially rewarding adventures of your life. It changes nearly everything you do, even the way you think. If you're to be successful and benefit from the experience, you must plan. In retirement every day is a "*day off*". You no longer have to think about what you are going to do on Monday. You no longer have to worry about what problems you will find on the job tomorrow. You're free to do as you wish. If you don't want to work any longer, and have the finances to do so, you don't have to work. However, if you want to work a few days each month, or even try a new job, you can that too. "*Retired. Don't want to. Don't need to. You can't make me.*" Retirement is a time to leave your previous work world behind, with its stresses, problems, deadlines and yes, even some of the people.

But it's also a time to look for a new direction, a new purpose, and a new outlook on life. You may want to travel to those places you've always wanted to visit, or put in a garden, enjoy your hobbies, paint the house, or move to a different part of the country - or the world. You may want to try out a different job on a part-time basis, start your own business, or get involved in all those things that you couldn't do when you were working full-time. Many retirees enroll in college courses, join volunteer groups, organize community events, and become social and political activists. During the first couple of years after they retire, they are so busy, they often wonder how they ever had time to work!

For others, retirement unfortunately evokes feelings of uselessness, of being *"put out to pasture"*. It's a sign of the *twilight years of life* and that *"old age"* is closing in. They feel unproductive, no longer useful or valued by what used to be their job, their friends, their families or colleagues. *"Yesterday I was the corporate boss. Now I'm nobody." "I used to be an engineer…a secretary…a teacher, but I'm not anymore."* In a society that frequently doesn't value older people and their wisdom, retirement can be a daunting experience. *"What do I do with the rest of my life? I'm not that old. I have a lot to offer and I know a lot more than these young kids do."*

The worst evil of all is to leave the ranks of the living before one dies. Seneca

Perhaps finances are a problem and there just isn't enough money coming in to meet your needs. That could mean you are forced into getting a job that you don't really want. While some people approach retirement from a negative stance, others look forward with a sense of anticipation. *"I'm going to volunteer with kids to help them learn to read." "I'm going to get involved in church groups and politics." "I can teach computer skills to older adults at the library." "I can get a part-time job at a supermarket."*

So now that you're going to be retired, exactly what *are* you going to do with the rest of your life? What happens next? What will you do with your time? Who will you see? What will you do with your days, your weeks and all of the years ahead of you? What will make you feel good about yourself and that you're contributing to the world around you as well as the people you care about the most?

You retire from a job. You keep a career for life.

A job can mean two things. It's where you work, but sometimes it means just something you do to get paid. It may or may not require formal education and can change from one place to another, depending on where you work. When you retire, the job ends. It was something you did to make a living. A career on the other hand, gives you an income, but it also gives you greater meaning and a sense of purpose. It is something you have pursued your entire life. It was something you were dedicated to and where you continually acquired new knowledge and skills. A career gives you lifelong knowledge and wisdom that you can now use in a variety of different settings and situations. If you were a teacher, you're still a teacher. You just may be teaching a different group of students. If you were a manager, you can still use those management skills in your community. If you were a pediatric nurse, friends will still ask you for health advice for their kids. You may not be employed as a plumber any longer, but you haven't forgotten your plumbing skills. It was something you did for years and you enjoyed. Finding a new direction, a new sense of purpose, and new goals for the years that follow retirement are essential to adjusting to retirement life and preparing for the years ahead.

It is the province of knowledge to speak.
And it is the privilege of wisdom to listen. "Oliver Wendell Holmes

Retirement is one of those transitions in life for which most people have had little practice, unless they've already retired once or twice before. And even then, there has to be a reason that they *"unretired"*. If you really think about it, when you retire, you have no experience for the *"job"*--but you have it anyway! And you are expected to be *successful* at it! Maybe the folks around you expect you to go fishing, play golf, travel, and enjoy doing absolutely nothing. These are often the same people who are working and wish they were also retired! Or maybe they *are* retired, and *really are doing nothing*. Other people cannot determine what *you* do and how *you* adjust. You can't fulfil their expectations. You must discover your own and set out on your own journey. While you need to involve other people, the decisions are still yours.

Reactions to retirement vary considerably from person to person, and even from one day to the next. It *is* a major transition to go from being employed to being *retired*. We've all seen the bumper stickers and cartoons. *"Retired and Gone Fishin"*. *"Buy an RV and Take the Dog"*. *"RV There Yet?"* *"I go where I'm Towed to."* *"No Alarm Clock, No Bedtime, No Money!"* *"Gainfully Unemployed."* Making this transition involves changes not only in your life but also in the lives of your friends, family members -"*your significant others*". Remember – no one lives totally in isolation. What affects you is bound to affect the people around you, whether you know it or not.

Your culture and ethnic background may also influence both your perceptions of retirement and the expectations of family members and friends. Perhaps it is assumed that your children will have major responsibilities for your care and welfare as you age. Perhaps you will be expected to provide care for the elders in your family. These matters need full consideration as you prepare for, and entre retirement.

> ***The only thing constant in life is change.***
> ***François de la Rochefoucauld***

An effective and healthy adjustment to retirement doesn't occur by accident. It takes thoughtful planning and considerable effort. You've probably put a lot of effort into having enough money and a big enough retirement income to be at least somewhat independent and do what you want. You've taken the time to fill out the forms to get your retirement or Social Security check, and made sure your Medicare forms were appropriately filed. But finances aren't everything. You can have an adequate income, plenty of investments, a nice home, and still be unhappy. There is much more to enjoying retirement than spending your money on new golf clubs, taking the RV to Florida for the winter, playing bridge on Wednesday nights, or lounging at the Senior Center. And just because Bingo is played in churches doesn't make it a religious experience! People usually pay much less attention to the intangible things that have a major impact on their ability to have a happy and well-adjusted retirement. Granted that a lot of folks are not prepared for the *financial* side of retirement, many are also not prepared for the psychological, or adjustment side. Adjusting to retirement means finding a new way of living, and unearthing those buried treasures that you have always valued in your "*self*" – but maybe haven't seen for a while.

Retirement requires handling changes in many of the roles you have had in life, changes in your relationships with other people, and who you look to for support. It creates changes in the very structure of your life, as well as sources for feeling good about yourself. It certainly changes how you use your time. These factors, these life pattern changes, are all interrelated, and together they create a much bigger picture than just looking at each one individually. Each change leads to more changes. And these changes affect not only you, but your family members, associates, friends, and even the people you used to work with. They influence how you are seen by others and how you view your own self. Retirement influences nearly every aspect of your life and the lives of those around you.

This book focuses on the adjustments and changes that can happen with retirement, and how you can meet these challenges successfully. It includes changes that your family and friends can anticipate, and how they might understand and handle them. Strategies are described throughout the book that you can use to plan for a future retirement or make changes for a more effective one if you are already retired. It's a new adventure in life, so talk about it, make a plan, and enjoy the journey. The chapters that follow will help you make your days more interesting and more rewarding. You will evaluate yourself, assess your interests, your likes and dislikes, your needs and your personal expectations. You will include the significant people in your life as you talk, create your plan and implement the changes you have chosen.

Life isn't over with retirement. A new life is just beginning.
Hit Your *"Now What? Button"*
Talk, Plan, and "Re-Tire"
Enter the New Retirement Age.

First, Let's Talk

The most basic of all human needs is the need
to understand and be understood.
The best way to understand people is to listen to them. Ralph Nichols

You have been talking, and *communicating* all of your life. You cried as a baby. You stomped your feet as a toddler. You talked back to your parents as a teenager. You answered the questions by your teachers and you talked about issues with your boss. You continue to talk with people. You use gestures when words don't work or you really need to make your point. You laugh, you grin, you wrinkle your forehead. You use body language to send messages and you constantly receive messages from others. You interpret these messages and act on what you heard, or what you felt. You use communication to share your thoughts, your ideas, your needs. Communication is a basic part of every human being and shares the person you are with others. You communicate with the people around you, your pets, and your world. The question is how good are you at it – at talking, and more importantly, at *communicating*?

After retirement you will *communicate* with people about issues, problems, needs, and activities that are different from what you talked about at work. Your focus will be on your new life, and maybe even new work roles, but not your previous job. Even if you work part-time, your focus will be different. Developing effective communication skills takes practice and a lot of ongoing effort. Really good skills promote positive interpersonal relationships. What you say, how you say it, and what you do when you are saying it, all convey messages to others. These messages not only give information with your words and behaviors, but they convey feelings – respect, love, disgust, concern, anger.

Being able to communicate effectively is an essential part of any meaningful relationship. All too frequently, minor sparks burst into open flames because two people are not communicating effectively. Perhaps someone is not listening. Perhaps someone is not interpreting meanings accurately, or perhaps words are being used to send mixed or insensitive messages.

If you have nothing to say, say nothing.
Mark Twain

Using communication skills *that work* can facilitate understanding and promote meaningful, healthy relationships. So what does this have to do with retirement? It means effectively communicating with the people around you about your retirement, talking about your plans, and discussing your reactions are essential parts of the adjustment process. It means that listening and incorporating the concerns and feelings of others into your plans and ideas are important not only for you, but for them. Couples and close friends do not always share the same visions about how one or both should adjust to retirement, - but sometimes they just don't talk about it. So here are some suggestions for those effective "*talks*".

Talking Points - Communication Techniques You Can Actually Use

What are you trying to say? What's the message you're trying to send? What do you really want to say? If you're feeling like, *"I'm not sure how I feel about retiring. Not sure I'm ready."* But instead you say, *"Ah, I'm not worried about retiring. I'll have plenty to do."* Then you're not being honest with yourself or the people around you. Are you sending the wrong message? Maybe you really don't know how you feel about retiring but haven't figured that out yet. Or maybe you just don't want to know yourself better.

Let's say you and your husband have been busy all day working on house repairs to get it ready to sell. You decide to fix a really nice dinner to celebrate all the changes you were able to get done. Then your husband makes it quite clear he doesn't like what you fixed and complains about everything on the table. Then you fire back with, *"You never like anything I fix for supper. You are so critical of everything I do."* What's happening here? You're striking back and making some pretty strong accusations that are most likely not even true. What could you have said that would be less argumentative? What if you just said, *"My feelings are hurt when you say things like that. What would you rather have had?"* Now you're sending a very different message. In any relationship, listening for the feelings and true meanings is important if the *real* message is to be understood. Listen to your own words. Examine your own feelings. And ask *"What am I really trying to say?"* - so you can prevent misunderstandings – and arguments.

Margery and Joe have been married for 35 years and are going to Joe's retirement dinner with co-workers.

Margery's Words: *"Joe, how do I look?"*

Margery's Thoughts: *"I sure hope he likes this dress. I got it just for the dinner tonight."*

Joe's Words: *"You look lovely, my dear, as always."*

Joe's Thoughts: *"An ugly brown color, but after this many years, I know better than to say that!"*

Of course, Joe knows that saying what he actually thinks would not exactly be the *smartest* thing he ever did. But rather than saying, *"You know, I'm glad you chose something special for tonight, but I really like that blue dress better"*. Or, *"I don't particularly like the color. I think the blue one looks better on you."* Otherwise, Joe's taking the *easy* way out. He's sending a clear message, but a very different one from what he's actually thinking. His words and thoughts are certainly not matching. Margery can probably sense that too. Let's face reality here, couples who have been married for 35 years really *can* read each other's thoughts! *So why lie?*

How are you trying to convey what you mean? Are you only using words? What messages are you sending with your facial expressions and body language? Is your body language saying something different from your words? Are saying what you really want to say? If your words and mannerism are sending opposite messages, you won't be accurately understood. Margery's interpretation of Joe's message:

Margery's Words: *"I thought you would like it."* (…oh really!!!)

Margery's Thoughts: *"I know that look. He thinks I look old and fat! And he hates this color. But he won't say anything."*

And she's right! But she's not telling him what she feels either.

What are you *really* saying? Do your words agree with your facial expressions and your gestures? If you're sending the message that you disagree, or you're angry, that may be very different from what you are saying. If you say *"That's O.K."*, but make an ugly face and walk out of the room, you're sending a different message. And the non-verbal message you're sending may be received much more strongly than your actual words. In fact, the person you're talking to may not even hear what you just said, but gets the expression on your face.

Margery, sensing something was wrong, returns to the topic:
Margery's Words: *"Are you sure you like it, Joe?"*
Margery's Actions: Turns around to show off her new dress.
Joe's Words: *"I said I did, didn't I? I'll go get the car."*

Now, Margery knows for sure - she was right!

In this situation, Joe, for some reason, is unwilling to share his actual feelings with Margery. Maybe that hasn't been a good idea in the past. Maybe he just doesn't want to get into an argument. Yet, he *is* sending his message. – the one he wants to send. Because his words don't say the same thing as his actions, he leaves Margery guessing, or does he? Although what he said doesn't match what he meant, she got the message anyway…!

What message was received? Did the other person hear you? Did the other person get the message you were trying to send or get a different message? Did you send more than one message and did the other person get a mixed message, or two or more, different messages? How do you know what message the other person received?

If you're saying something, or you think you are, and somebody is receiving an entirely different message, you cause communication meltdown which can quickly lead to even more conflict. Check with the person you're talking with and clarify what you said and what the other person heard. *"Tell me what you heard me say." "Tell me what I just said." "Tell me what you think I just said."* This clarifies messages and helps to prevent misunderstandings.

And now, Margery and Joe are in the car.

Joe: *"They decided the retirement dinner would be at Dorman's Grill this year. That's not where we usually go, but should be great."*
Margery: *"But we always go to Lennon's Restaurant for the retirement dinners. I thought we were going there again."*
Joe: *"But I thought you said they should decide where to go."* Now sounding a bit angry, *"So where did you want to go?"*

Margery: *"I thought I said Lennon's Restaurant, where we always go for retirement dinners. That's a tradition. What did you hear me say?"*

Obviously there is miscommunication going on. There have probably been problems for a long time. This is just a repeat of past behavior. But Margery is now trying to get clarification from Joe about what she said.

What response did you get? What did the other person say back to you? What facial expressions or body movements did you see in response to what you said, or did? Did you get the response you expected? Is the behavior of the other person consistent with his words?

Joe: *"You said Lennon's Restaurant. I thought the folks at work were supposed to decide where we were going. I said that Dorman's might be nice for a change. I hear they have excellent food and service. Lennon's was not all that great last time, as I recall."*

What is the message you got from the words? How are you interpreting the message that has just been sent to you? If messages aren't understood, *"talking"* may help. Check out what you think you heard, or saw, so you can understand. This helps you get the message accurately, rather than possibly relying on any misinterpretation you have made. *"What I heard you say was..." "The frown on your face said... to me."*

What Bugs People?

Bob and Louise have been married for nearly 40 years. Bob just retired from his job as an engineer. He and Louise have been planning to travel extensively after retirement; however, Bob was forced to take an early retirement and his retirement pay is less than they had counted on. They're now discussing how many trips they can plan during the next couple years and who they will visit. Bob wants to buy an RV and go south for three months during each winter to get away from the cold weather. Louise would rather spend the time visiting their two children and their families.

Bob: *"I don't see why we have to go see the kids. They have money. Let them come see us. They can come here when we're home and not traveling."*
Louise: *"You just don't care about the kids any more. And, an RV is expensive. It costs way too much money and we don't have that kind of money to spend."*

Bob: *"I care about the kids, but it's my retirement money and I'll do with it what I want to."*

Marilyn: *"It's my money, too. After all, I took care of you, the kids and the house all of these years. And you didn't do anything to help."*

Comments:

Bob is expressing his feelings, but also venting his hostility about the kids having their own money and his right to control the money – *his* money – after retirement. Louise responds by putting down Bob about not caring about the kids. She then changes to negative comments about money. She doesn't respond to his comments. Bob, in turn defends his caring about the kids and tries to exert control over the money. Louise defends her right to the money and how she has contributed. Then she brings up old baggage by accusing Bob of not helping all of those years. In all of this, there is no evidence either one of them is actually understanding the other person. They're not thinking about what they are saying or how anything should be said it – in a constructive manner. Not only that, but if they are communicating this way now, chances are pretty good they have been doing it that way for many years. This is not new behavior. It is a repeat of previous interactions between the two of them.

Did You Know?

Retirees who are forced to retire may have a significantly lower sense of well-being.

Source: Bender, K. (2012). An analysis of well-being in retirement: The role of pensions, health and voluntariness of retirement, *The Journal of Socio-Economics, 41*(4), 424-433.

Some may find that retirement actually improves their psychological well-being.

Source: Latif, E. (2011). The impact of retirement on psychological well-being in Canada. *The Journal of Socio-Economics, 40*(4) Aug, 373-380.

What <u>Do</u> I Say?

Now let's revisit Bob and Louise.

<u>Bob</u>: *"I don't see why we have to go see the kids. Let's call them and ask when they might be able to come here. Then let's talk about where we can go."*
<u>Louise</u>: *"Great idea. I agree. After we talk to the kids, let's talk about how much money we have to spend and what's workable."*
<u>Bob</u>: *"I would really like to rent or buy an RV and go to Texas for a couple of months in January and February just to get away from the cold weather. What do you think about that idea?"*
<u>Louise</u>: *"A travel camper sounds terribly expensive. Do you know how much it would cost? And what about the cost of gas and rental spaces?"*
<u>Bob</u>: *"No, but I can check several Internet sites and get some estimates."*
<u>Louise</u>: *"If it is too expensive, maybe we could look at what other options might be. Maybe we could rent an apartment or a house on a short term basis."*

Comments:

Bob and Marilyn are now responding to what is being said, rather than reacting with their own negative agendas. The communication is direct, positive, and open without putting down the other person. They are throwing out ideas, options to consider and to discuss. Try to listen to what other people are saying to you. Learn to disagree with ideas and concepts instead of rejecting the person who is making them.

I accept you but I don't have to accept your behavior or your ideas.

How Do We Talk About This?

Don't be the *"Historical Pack Rat"*

Avoid revisiting everything you can remember that you think somebody has done wrong for the past thirty years! *"Remember in 1968 when we were on vacation and you got us lost for two hours in Chicago?"* Your first thought is, *"No.!"* Or, *"Yes, and it bugs me when you keep bringing it up over and over."* Excess baggage is heavy to keep carrying around. Past years and past events are long gone and can't be changed now. If there are remaining feelings, then deal with the *remnants*. And then – <u>*Move On!*</u>

Travel light in life. Excess baggage comes with a surcharge.

You can't live in the past. While your memories are important to you, they may not be important to everybody else. Things are different today and nobody probably cares what you did. You can't use yesterday's standards to tell people what to do today or to judge them. It rarely works to say, *"When I was young...we did so and so."* This really bugs younger people. You aren't young and your values may be very different from others now. What's important is what's going on now.

Be careful about telling your adult children how to raise their kids. When you were a teenager, you didn't have fast food restaurants, computers, the Internet, mobile phones and illegal drugs. Chances are, if you were a parent, your children didn't have these things either. Coping with all of these changes is difficult for parents today, and their world is very different from what yours was. If you want to talk *historically*, and share what the world and your life were like when you were growing up, that's fine. Family and friends might find that interesting. It also helps them have a sense of the past and appreciate family history. It's a way of passing down information to the next generation. But that's different from trying to set standards and influence values based on what you did 60 years ago. The world has changed...and it keeps changing. You have to learn to change with it. This doesn't mean, however, that you have to compromise your own beliefs and values just to please those around you.

The young people you meet have never used a typewriter, a dial phone, or a 33 1/3 record, and have never heard of "I Love Lucy" or "The Ed Sullivan Show".

Listen for feelings, not just the words.
The feelings that you get from another person are frequently a much more accurate reading of what's really being communicated than the words are. Too often people get caught up in the words, and reactions to those words. They miss the opportunity to look for the feelings behind the words.
Respond to the feelings and non-verbal behaviors you are getting.

If you respond to the feelings as well as the words, you are responding to the whole message, rather than just the words that may be cluttering up the communication. Remember, the feelings you are getting are strong clues within your own self about the messages that are being sent. Listen to them.

Make facial expressions and body language consistent with the words you are saying.

When you say, *"You look sharp today,"* be sure that's what you mean.

But also, say the words with a smile and a gesture that convey the same thing as the words.

Check with other people to see if what you heard, or felt, was the message that they were really trying to send.

"What I felt you said was, you don't like it when I don't tell you I'll be late getting home." We've all said things, and looked at somebody, who was looking back with an expressions that said - *"What on earth are you talking about?"* That invisible, but clearly obvious, question mark above somebody's head is a clue something needs to be fixed with the conversation.

How Do I Criticize and Make It Feel Good, - or at Least OK?

Talk to the person *directly*.

If you have a problem with your husband, your wife, or a friend, telling the guy at work or somebody at the gym might make you feel better – for the moment – but it's not going to solve the problem. Deal directly with the person involved. Try to talk about what's going on. If you can't agree, then *agree to disagree*, and *Move On. Really* move on, not just say you're going to and then keep bringing up the issue as *old baggage*.

One of the most important achievements in life is when you've learned how to let go and move on.

Take care of the situation *when it happens*. If you are having a problem with somebody, take care of it as soon as possible to prevent a buildup of harmful energy. If there are other people present, and it wouldn't be appropriate to discuss the issue right then, wait until you are out of the situation to resolve the problem. At least have a private conversation.

Waiting two or three weeks afterwards will make it difficult for both of you to remember exactly what was said and exactly what happened. As a result, you increase the likelihood of remembering incorrectly, misinterpreting comments and exaggerating the situation. You may even have forgotten what happened, when the other person didn't. This really complicates things.

Be *specific* - and be *constructive.* Saying *"You don't do anything right"* is not only inflammatory, but it can't possibly be true! If you didn't like that your wife went shopping all afternoon, simply say, *"I don't like it when you go shopping all afternoon when we have other things that needed to get done."* rather than *"You're never home when you should be,"* or *"You're always out shopping when we have work to do."* Hostile and demeaning doesn't work!

In most cases, anything that needs to be said, can be said in a constructive manner. Rather than saying, *"That shirt looks awful with those slacks."* You might say, *"I believe that new green and white shirt you bought would go better with those slacks than that one does."* Positive comments are received more willingly, more positively, and more constructively than those that are unnecessarily critical.

Be sure you're right *before* you speak. Let's say you thought your husband was supposed to be home at four o'clock. But he not only told you he wouldn't be home until six, but he left you a note on the kitchen table that said so. For whatever reason, you didn't hear what he said and you didn't read the note. You're probably going to incite a small riot when he gets home a little before six and you chew him out for being late. This puts you on an unnecessary *guilt trip* - first for not listening or reading the note, and second for *being wrong*!

> *False words are not only evil in themselves, but*
> *they infect the soul with evil. Socrates*

Talk about what is happening *now.* Once again, bringing up the last twenty or thirty years' worth of "*baggage*" will turn off anybody. If you're in a disagreement, try to avoid giving an *historical summation* of everything you didn't like about the person for the past two decades. *"Yeah, I remember when we were at the kid's house in 1984 and you spilled beets on their new white table cloth."* Things that happened thirty years ago can't be changed today - only the feelings can. Bringing up the *"garbage list"* puts the person you're talking with on the defense. And besides, you're probably just trying to make the other person look bad, rather than resolve the problem. Of course, having a sense of humor also helps. You may now be able to laugh about the beets on the table cloth and the ensuing events. *"I have never seen you scramble so fast. And then when I tried to help clean it up, I dumped Jimmy's glass of chocolate milk off the table and it landed on that hairy dog they had."* Sharing humorous times from the past can be fun and is quite different from bringing up old, unsolved issues that demean and control somebody else.

Own your *own* words. Say what *you* feel and what *you* believe. Starting sentences with "I" sets the stage for communicating *your* ideas. *"I wish you would have stopped at the store on your way home and picked up the dog food"* is considerably more constructive than, *"Why didn't you pick up dog food on your way home? You knew we were out this morning."* Why is demanding an explanation for somebody else's behavior. *You* is finger-pointing and blaming, rather than dealing with the issue.

How do I Avoid Inciting a Riot?

Saying things to make the other person look bad is not constructive. *"You don't know what you're talking about."* We've all heard that one. Your real motivation here is to put down the other person or put somebody in a *"bad light"* compared to yourself. While it's intended to elevate you, it rarely does. Whatever the reason, it can be unkind and move discussions in a negative direction.

Demanding an Explanation from Others

"Why did you do that?" *"Why did you say that?"* How often we hear those words! Yet they really can do a lot of harm. Generally speaking, using *"why"* questions actually block communication. Most people feel that they have been put on the defense. *"Why?"* is translated to mean *"Defend yourself"* or, *"Defend what you said."* Rather than helping someone talk about what happened, what was said, it makes people feel threatened so they get hostile and fight back. Instead, try using statements like, *"Tell me about that"*. These words open the opportunity for dialogue. But remember, when you say *"Tell me about it"* - then keep quiet and

listen - without interrupting - and without criticism. You have invited conversation…take the opportunity to listen.

If speaking is silver, then listening is gold." Turkish Proverb

Giving Approval for Unacceptable Behavior

Janet had a terrible headache. The grandkids were visiting and playing in the family room. Suddenly, she yelled at them for leaving their toys all over and cracker crumbs on the sofa. They got upset and started crying. Her husband looks at her and says, *"That's O.K. dear. You weren't feeling well. I know you didn't mean it."* Maybe Janet didn't feel well, and maybe she didn't mean it, but when her husband makes excuses for her, it gives a stamp of approval for her inappropriate behavior. *"Janet, when you're not feeling well and get angry, if you wait a little while before you say anything, you usually handle the situation better."* This acknowledges the behaviors, and the fact she didn't feel well, but gives Janet some constructive, positive suggestions for change in future interactions with the grandkids.

Being Defensive When threatened, a natural response is to defend. Yet, being defensive does not usually result in the resolution of conflicts.

Janet to her husband William: *"Why are you washing the car? You were supposed to mow the lawn today."*

William: *"What do you mean, why am I washing the car? Because it's dirty, that's why!"*

Of course, this has nothing to do with mowing the lawn. And Janet is trying to make him feel guilty for not mowing the lawn. Her comments take on considerably different meaning with different words.

Janet: *"I thought that we agreed you would mow the lawn today rather than wash the car."*

William: *"I know, but the car was filthy. I'll mow the lawn as soon as I finish."*

Using Clichés

"Everything will be O.K." "It'll be alright." "That's alright." "It'll all work out for the best." We hear these comments all too often - after a serious accident, when somebody dies, when there's a house fire, when you get divorced, etc. etc. etc. Although there are times when these comments are

indeed reassuring, especially to a small child, they convey a message of *"I can make everything better." "I didn't know what else to say."* Or, *"If I say it will be O.K., then it will be O.K. – and I don't have to face the situation"* If it won't be O.K., or if you don't know that it will, then don't say it will be O.K. In fact, you are better off if you don't say anything. The touch of a hand and a hug can mean a great deal more.

> ### *Many attempts to communicate are nullified by saying too much." Robert Greenleaf*

Remember, the person who is receiving the words may be feeling, *"Then why does it hurt so bad right now?"* Or, *"I don't know that it's going to be O.K." "He's dead. He won't be here anymore. I'm alone now."* Again, if you don't know what else to say, don't say anything. Or just say *"I understand"*. Just a *"Tell me how you are feeling"* can go a lot further. This allows the other person to talk about what *he or she* feels - rather than listening to how *you* feel.

If you keep talking long enough, the room will grow empty.

Disapproving of Others

"You never do anything around here." Never sure is a long time and your words say, *"I don't value you or what you do, and I'm going to make sure you know it"*. There is a great deal of difference between what a person says or does and who the person is as a human being. Learning to disapprove of someone's behaviors without disapproving of the person can be difficult and exhausting. Yet, it is an essential element in establishing meaningful, caring, loving relationships. *"I don't like what you just did."* Or, *"I don't like what you just said"* is very different from *"I don't like you"*.

Telling Somebody Else What to Do

"You really should see your mother more often. She raised you and now you don't even care about her." You immediately think, *"Says who? You? And who are you to tell me what I should or shouldn't do? And who I care about?"* Most people don't really want advice and the person who asks for it the *most* probably wants it the *least*. *"Shoulds"* and *"You ought to..."* have started a lot of arguments. Your message is: *"I'm going to tell you what to*

do. And I know better what's good for you than you do." "I can control what you do." Well, just who made you the authority? What right do you have to tell anybody else, adult that is, what to do?

Once we become adults we have the right to freedom of choice and to self-determination. We have the *right* to make our own decisions - even if they turn out to be disastrous and cause grief. Acknowledging that adults have the right to make their own choices, even when you disagree with them or feel they are wrong, also acknowledges that they have the power over their own decisions and lives. Speak for yourself. *"With your health history, I am concerned that you do not get an annual physical exam."* Now you're speaking for yourself, and encouraging the other person to make a decision.

> ***Trying to put words back in your mouth is like trying to put toothpaste back in the tube.***

Changing the Subject

Let's say you are at a church picnic and are in the middle of a discussion with your sister and some friends about the selection of a new pastor. You say, *"I think Rev. Richards has a lot to offer. He's young, energetic and seems really interested in this church"*. Your sister keeps on eating her fried chicken and says, *"You know I think I'll make an apple pie for the bake sale on Tuesday. What do you think?"*

What you *think* is, *"Apple pie? Bake sale?* What does *that* have to do with the anything?" *Nothing!!* Your sister's comments suggest that she was not listening or, at least, she was more interested in what *she* was thinking about than what *the group* was saying. Changing the subject devalues the contributions of the person you are talking with. If you want to change the subject, listen first to what the other person is saying and attend to that. Simple statements can then move the discussion to a new topic, while being attentive to the current one - and without devaluing anyone else's comments. *"Yes, I think he's got a lot to offer. I'd like to change the subject to the bake sale for a moment. Can we do that? I need suggestions for what I should take."*

How do We Work This Out?

No matter how effective, caring, and attentive we try to be in communicating with others, there will be conflicts - some trivial and some overwhelming. Learning how to manage conflicts, how to resolve them, and how to move on, are necessary for the continued growth of any relationship. And every relationship takes work - some more than others! Here are a few suggestions.

Listen *FIRST,* Then Speak

Ever notice that when two people are arguing, they are usually both trying to talk (or yell) at the same time! This means, *nobody is listening.* Someone has to listen – FIRST - if the conversation is going to go anywhere productive. Somebody has to start the listening process. Many arguments can be prevented by, *"Tell me about that."* or *"You seem upset. Tell me what's going on."* But then you have an obligation to listen to what the other person is saying. Try being the *first one* to listen. Listen to what someone is saying to you - listen for words and listen for feelings. Then think about what you heard, what you felt, and the message you received. *Then talk.*

Don't *Interrupt*

Nothing is more annoying in a discussion [or worse yet in an argument] than to have someone who is constantly interrupting every time you try to say something. You probably know someone who has to constantly finish your sentences – *before* you can. And frequently what the other person says has nothing to do with what you were going to say. This is different, however from a couple, or friends who have been together for 50 years and instinctively know what the other person is going to say. Interrupting sends a strong message that *"What I have to say is more important than what you have to say"*. Avoid the temptation and listen instead. Control yourself! Then expect the other person to listen to you. And be open about it if there is a problem. *"I have listened to your comments, now I would like for you to listen to mine."* Most adults learned as kids that interrupting someone who is speaking, or *"butting in"* or *"barging in"* as it was called, was considered rude. We may not have been taught it was *"ineffective communication"*, but it was definitely *rude*. Yet when people grow up, they seem to feel that rule only applied when they were kids! The *"barger-inner"* is the person who must always speak when he wants to say something, important or not. This is the person who is constantly cutting into conversations to add a comment, to change the subject, or just say something to turn the attention to him (or her, obviously).You know somebody like that. Their response is, *"I was just being friendly"*. *"I thought we were having a give and take conversation. I wasn't butting in"*. It may not be an attempt to be friendly, but rather to demand the attention of everyone else. Avoid the temptation to "butt in" and wait until others are finished, or at least ask if you can comment.

Look for the *REAL* Message

Listen for the *real* message someone is trying to send you. Is your wife upset because you didn't pick up the newspapers off the floor, *or* is she upset that you don't show enough concern for her and what she does for *you*? Are your kids mad because you want to visit them for Thanksgiving, *or* that they value their privacy and want to spend the holiday with their own kids? The words somebody says may not be what's actually going on. So try to figure it out, and if you can't – just ASK.

Speak for *Yourself*, Not the Whole World

It is certainly presumptuous when somebody says, "Well, everybody is doing it" or "The whole family thinks we should…" Unless you have polled *everybody* and are authorized to speak for *everybody* you can't possible know how *everybody* feels. Using these global phrases is more of an attempt to legitimize what you want or believe than it is to reflect the opinion of others. It says that you believe your opinion alone is not sufficient and you need the consensus of *everybody* to give credence and authority to what you are saying. It's called the *"power in numbers approach"*. Are you trying to control what other people think or what they want? Speak only for yourself and how *you* feel. Other people really can speak for themselves! And if you *must* speak for *everybody*, be certain you know how *everybody* feels and that you are truly reflecting *their* opinions, not just your own and using other people to control what you want to happen.

> *Everything we hear is an opinion, not a fact. Everything we see is a perspective, not the truth. Marcus Aurelius*

Is this really any of MY business?

Sometimes it's easier to think we can solve *other* people's problems, rather than working on our *own*. Ever think you knew *exactly* what somebody else should do if you could just convince him of that? Of course you have. You think you have the enlightened and right answer for somebody's problems. In other words, you figure the other person isn't capable of finding his own answers – the answers you want him to have. You're trying to make someone else's decisions. This kind of interference can cause a lot of unrest, as well as unnecessary grief for both of you. Being supportive, showing caring and concern, and allowing the other person to share feelings and ideas can lead to problem solving without you trying to control someone else's decisions. Ask yourself, *"Is this really any of my business?"* If not, keep out! And keep quiet! *Unless, of course, it's unethical, immoral or illegal.* And then make sure you're still not trying to impose your own values. And, be sure the other person *wants* your opinion.

Other questions to ask, *"Is this my problem or is this your problem? If it's not my problem, then why am I getting into it? What am I trying to gain by this? What am I risking?"* Sometimes people feel they just have to solve everybody else's problems, but the other person may not appreciate having someone butt in. Give people the chance to solve their own problems. Every adult has the freedom to make choices, to make decisions, and has to live with the consequences. Unfortunately, sometimes the rest of us also have to live with the problems that result from those decisions. But that's the reality of life and living with others.

Be Open and Willing to Change

Change is inevitable. This is one of the truths of time that we can rely on. Events and people change our lives. Sometimes they bring happiness and sometimes they bring grief. New people enter our inner circle and others leave. As you age, there will be many changes. Retirement brings a new set of changes - moving to a new home or community, finding new friends, leaving friends and changing the way you live. Downsizing a home means giving up things you cherish. Retirees often say that this is the most difficult thing they have to do when moving to a retirement community. Getting rid of personal, valued possessions is difficult. It's tough to decide what goes with you and what doesn't. Do the kids want things? Do they even want the things you want to give them? Remember, they are from a different era and just because you cherished something, doesn't mean that they will. What are your other options? What can you sell? What can you give away? What can you donate to Goodwill, the Salvation Army, your church yard sale? Talk with your family and friends. Let them help you with these decisions. It will make it a lot easier.

Coping with the many changes of life is simply a part of being human – sometimes they challenge our resilience and our ability to adapt. Resistance to change, when it is really needed however, not only slows progress in life, but can lead to unhealthy ways of adapting. Change begets change. It fosters new ideas, new issues, and sometimes creates new problems, but remains a fundamental component in life's journey. Trying to keep things *"the way they are"* may feel secure, but it is may not be in your best interest, or the best interest of those around you. Change in itself is usually not the problem. It's the outcomes that are. Making wise decisions leading to change, and then accepting and adjusting to them are paramount for meaningful progress. Look carefully at your options. Think about the consequences. Which are positive and which are negative? Make a list. Which list is longer and more beneficial? What consequences will have the greatest impact on you? On other people? Can you really adjust to the outcomes?

If you don't like something change it; if you can't change it,
change the way you think about it. Mary Engelbreit

Resolve the Issue and *Move On*

Consistent with junking the *"old baggage"*, is the idea of fixing problems of the present and moving on. Then issues don't become old baggage. As we said earlier, when a problem arises, the sooner it can be resolved, the sooner both people can move on and get on with other matters. Check with others to see if it is resolved. *"Are you O.K. with this?" "Have we resolved this? Can we move on now?"* This can be really tough to do at times, especially when it involves major problems that caused a lot of pain. Some of these issues never get fully resolved, like the loss of a family member. You simply learn to accept what has happened. That doesn't mean you have to forget what happened. But that's different from the daily nagging stuff. Revisiting issues suggests that maybe they have really not been resolved. If they aren't, try again, but there is always a time to let it go. Once you have *agreed* the matter is closed, *leave it closed.*

> **When one door closes, another opens; but we often look so long and so regretfully upon the closed door that we do not see the one which has opened for us. Alexander Graham Bell**

Situations

Read each of the situations listed in the following. Then figure out what you would say differently. What would your response be? What nonverbal messages would you try to send?

Dialogue between Harry and George

Harry and George have been friends since childhood and live fairly close to each other in a small rural farming town. They go fishing together about once a week in the summer and even belong to many of the same organizations in the community. They know each other very well and usually agree on most things except politics. Harry has decided that his house needs to be painted on the outside and he wants to do it himself to save money. Now that he's retired, he has the time. He asks George to help and George agrees. Since neither one of them has ever painted a house, they each ask a couple friends for some advice. On Saturday, George goes to Harry's house and they begin to plan how they will tackle the job. Based on the advice they have received they immediately get into a hot argument over how they are going to go about it.

Harry: *"We need to start with the windows and trim. I'll do the front of the house and you start on the windows on the porch."*

George: *"We can't do the windows and the trim until the house is painted. We won't know if the trim color goes with the house. And besides, we could get house paint on the trim."*

Harry: *"You can't do the house first. The trim paint will get on the house. You have to do the trim first."*

George: *"Well, I'm not doing the trim first. If that's what you want, you do the damn trim yourself. I'm outta here."*

Harry: *"Well, it's my house and I say how we do it. So go home. I don't need your help anyway."*

1. What would you have said or done differently?
2. What would you say in response to the last comments by both George and Harry?

The single biggest problem in communication is the illusion that it has taken place." George Bernard Shaw

Dialogue between Sarah and Jeff

Sarah lives in Virginia and her brother Jeff lives in Utah. Both are retired. They have been planning for a couple of years to get together *"someplace in between"*. Sarah's son Michael has just called and said that he is being transferred and that he and his family are moving to Nashville. They will have a large house and plenty of room for Sarah and Jeff if they would like to visit. Sarah says that she thinks this is a wonderful idea and it would give her a chance to see her three grandchildren as well. Cost would be a lot less than a motel. Jeff has some other trips he wants to plan and calls Sarah to discuss their reunion. The following conversation takes place.

Jeff: *"Sarah, I thought we needed to talk about when and where we can get together this summer."*
Sarah: *"Oh, I have it all solved. Michael and his wife have invited us to come to Nashville after they get moved in. They have plenty of room. I told them we would be there by July 4 and probably stay until the 15th."*
Jeff: *"I would have preferred that you had talked with me before telling them that we were coming."*
Sarah: *"I didn't have time. Now you'll need to take your golf clubs. Michael is an avid golfer, you know, and he's very good. You'll probably need to do some practicing before you'll want play a round with him."*
Jeff: *"Sarah, I would rather not meet in Nashville, and I certainly do not want to stay with Michael and his family. That would not be a vacation for me."*
Sarah: (Sarah begins to cry.) *"You don't want me to see my grandkids. You don't care about me like you did when we were young. You never want to do what I want to do."*

What would you have said or done differently? What's really going on here?

Dialogue between Jack and Martha

Jack and Martha have been owners of an appliance store for over 25 years and have decided it's time to retire. They have three grown children and one of them, their daughter, wants to take over the store. She lives in the same town and has worked there periodically for several years. The other two kids are college graduates, have good jobs but live across the country. Jack and Martha have to determine what they will do with the store. Jack wants to sell it and Martha wants it to go to their only daughter. The following conversation takes place.

<u>Jack</u>: *"I don't think Elsa has the education or the financial skills to run the store. She never went to college and is basically lazy."*

<u>Martha</u>: *"She's not lazy and you don't have a college education either. So what's the problem? She can do anything she wants to."*

<u>Jack</u>: *"Just because I don't have a college education doesn't mean that I don't understand finances. We've done pretty well on our own and I'm the one who ran the financial end of this deal."*

<u>Martha</u>: *"Well, I ran the store while you in the back office playing with your computer and data sheets."*

<u>Jack</u>: *"The two boys should have something to say about this. If she takes over the store that means she will inherit it and they will get nothing."*

1. What are the problems with this communication?
2. What would you say differently?
3. If you were in this situation, how would you propose resolving the conflict?

CHAPTER 1

ASSESSING WHERE YOU ARE

The first step in working through any new adjustment is to figure out where you are. And you need this step if you're going to plan what you're going to do after you retire. Fill out the following questionnaire. Use the Pre-Retirement Assessment if you *are not yet retired*. If you're already retired, you can do the Post-Retirement Assessment. Go someplace where you can be alone and think. Then fill it out. Be honest! You have nothing to lose and a lot to gain.

After you have done that, take the filled out assessment to someone who knows you well – and you trust. This could be a close friend, might be your wife or husband, your partner or could even be one of your kids. If you're married, there is a section you and your spouse should discuss together. The important thing is that you go through each item on the assessment and talk about it. Get feedback from others on how they see your answers. Then, discuss your differences. And be prepared for differences! This is where those communication skills we talked about earlier will come in handy! This is a great time for you and your wife or husband, your partner, your friend to talk about your different perceptions and what retirement is going to mean for each of you...yes each of you. Remember, your retirement affects everybody around you.

Then, once again find a place where you can think and go over what you discussed. This is about exploring your own beliefs and feelings and, getting input from someone else about your ideas and retirement plans.

Others may not see you as you do. It would be pretty unusual if they did. Others may not view your retirement the same way that you do. Having a *"window"* to see yourself can provide meaningful information about where you are in your planning as well as your future adjustment to retirement. It can tell you how other people might adjust to all the changes. What impact is your retirement going to have on them? You don't have to agree, but it will give you some idea about what they're thinking and what they are looking forward to, as well as what bothers them the most.

Review the concepts in Chapter 1 on communication and conflict. If you skipped Chapter 1, go back and read it before moving on. You will then be ready to begin looking at the things you would like to change. The next few chapters are designed to help you look at what is currently going on and help you develop strategies to move forward.

Pre-Retirement Assessment

Check (✓) the answer that best describes you.

1. How do you feel about retiring? __ I'm eagerly looking forward to it __ I'm sort of looking forward to it __ I'm not sure about retirement __ I'm not looking forward to it __ I'm dreading retirement	4. If you don't exercise at all, what are the reasons? __ Too many health problems __ Don't want to __ No time __ No one to exercise with __ It's boring __ Can't afford it or no equipment __ Other _____
2. How do you feel about your job right now? __ I greatly enjoy my job __ I sort of enjoy my job __ I'm not sure how I feel about my job __ I don't enjoy my job __ I hate my job	5. How would you rate your health? __ Excellent __ Above average __ Good __ Fair __ Poor
3. On an average, how many hours a week do you do volunteer work in your community? __ None __ 5 hours or less __ 6-10 hours __ 11-15 hours __ 16-20 hours __ More than 20 hours	6. Who are the people you count on in a crisis? __ Spouse or partner __ Co-workers __ Family other than spouse or partner __ Friends __ Religious leaders/friends __ Don't count on anybody else

7. What is the average number of hours you exercise <u>each week</u>? __ I don't exercise __ At least 30 minutes __ 1-2 hours __ 3-4 hours __ 4-5 hours __ 6 hours or more	11. Do You Have a Pet? __ Yes, a member of the family __ Yes, but would rather not have one __ No, but would like one __ No, and do not want one. __ No, not allowed where I live
8. Do you have a computer? __ Yes, and know how to use it well __ Yes, but not good at using it __ No, and have no need for one __ No, but would like to get one	12. How far away are your closest *independently living* relatives? __ Live in same city __ Within 50 miles __ Over 50 miles __ Do not have close relatives
9. If you have a computer, what do you use it for? __ Do work at my business or workplace __ Do work in my home office __ Send e-mail __ Get on the Internet __ Play games __ Personal education __ Other (List _____)	13. How far away are your closest *independently living* friends? __ Live in same city __ Within 50 miles __ Over 50 miles __ Do not have close friends
10. What is the role of religion or spirituality in your life? __ Very important __ Sometimes important __ Not very important __ Not important at all	14. What are your plans for working after your retirement? __ Do not plan to work __ Plan to get a new job __ Plan to work part-time __ Plan to start a new career __ Have not decided on work plans

15. What is your current involvement in volunteer or community organizations? __ Very involved __ Sometimes involved __ Rarely involved __ Not involved at all	17. How would you assess your finances for what you plan to do after you retire? __ Sufficient to meet my/our needs __ Marginal but sufficient to meet my/our needs __ Insufficient to meet my/our needs __ Have no idea
16. What are your plans for relocating after retirement? __ Plan to move to another part of the country __ Plan to move to a different home in same area __ Do not plan to move __ Have not decided whether to relocate	18. Do you have hobbies that you enjoy doing? __ Yes, and do on a regular basis __ Yes but rarely do them __ Do not have hobbies

Directions: Check (✓) your response to each of the following statements that most closely describes your **beliefs about retirement**. Use this key:

SA=Strongly Agree   A=Agree   U=Undecided
D=Disagree   SA=Strongly Disagree

STATEMENTS	SA	A	U	D	SD
1. I know what retirement will be like for me.					
2. I will have plenty of things to do that I enjoy.					
3. I will enjoy being active.					
4. I will feel good about myself.					
5. I will have people to rely upon when problems occur.					
6. I will enjoy retirement.					
7. I have plans for I will do with my time after I retire.					
8. I will get up at the same time as I did before I retired.					
9. Other people will say that I am happily retired.					
10. I will rarely feel lonely.					
11. A pet will be an important part of my life.					
12. I will have friends to associate with on a regular basis.					
13. I will have sufficient financial resources to meet my basic needs.					
14. People will regularly visit my home.					
15. I have plans to prevent me from becoming bored.					
16. I will enjoy life more after I am retired.					
17. Other people will tell me what to do.					
18. My living standards will decline after I retire.					
19. I worry about my future after retirement.					
20. I am adequately prepared for retirement.					

21. I think depression could be a problem for me.					
22. Adjusting to retirement will be easy for me.					
23. I worry about my health as I get older.					
24. Retirement will be easier for me after I have been retired for a while.					
IF MARRIED or HAVE PARTNER					
25. My spouse/partner and I will switch some roles after I retire.					
26. My marriage will be more satisfying after I retire.					
27. My spouse/partner and I will get along better after I retire.					
28. I will sometimes feel in the way around the house.					
29. My spouse/partner and I will have better sexual relations after I retire.					
30. My spouse/partner will say I am around the house too much.					
31. My spouse/partner and I look forward to retirement.					
32. My spouse/partner and I will have to spend too much time together.					
33. My culture and ethnic background will impact my retirement.					

Post-Retirement Assessment

Check (✓) the answer that best describes you.

1. How do you feel about being retired? __ I really enjoy retirement __ I sort of enjoy retirement __ I'm not sure how I feel about retirement __ I do not enjoy retirement __ I really dislike retirement	4. If you don't exercise at all, what are the reasons? __ Health problems __ Not interested __ No time __ No one to exercise with __ It's boring __ Can't afford or no equipment __ Other
2. How do you feel about your last job? __ I really enjoyed my last job __ I sort of enjoyed my last job __ I'm not sure how I feel about my last job __ I did not enjoy my last job __ I hated my last job	5. How would you rate your health? __ Excellent __ Above average __ Good __ Fair __ Poor
3. What is your current working for pay status? __ I'm retired and do not want to work __ I'm retired and working part-time __ I'm retired and now working full-time __ I'm looking for full or part-time work	6. Who are the people you count on in a crisis? __ Spouse/partner __ Former co-workers __ Family other than spouse/partner __ Friends __ Don't count on anybody else

7. On an average, how many hours a week do you do volunteer work in your community?

__ None
__ 5 hours or less
__ 6-10 hours
__ 11-15 hours
__ 16-20 hours
__ More than 20 hours

8. Do you have a computer?

__ Yes, and know how to use it well
__ Yes, but not good at using it
__ No, and have no need for one
__ No, but would like to get one

9. If you have a computer, what are the primary reasons you use it?

__ Do work at my business or workplace
__ Do work in my home office
__ Send e-mail
__ Get on the Internet
__ Play games
__ For my personal education

10. Do You Have a Pet?

__ No, but would like one
__ No, and do not want one
__ No, not allowed where I live
__ Yes

11. How far away are your closest *independently living* relatives?

__ Live in same town or city
__ Within 50 miles
__ Over 50 miles
__ Do not have close relatives

12. How far away are your closest *independently living* friends?

__ Live in same town or city
__ Within 50 miles
__ Over 50 miles
__ Do not have close friends

13. What is the role of religion or spirituality in your life?

__ Very important
__ Sometimes important
__ Not very important
__ Not important at all

16. Did you return to work or start a new career after retirement?

__ Did not return to work
__ Work full time
__ Work part-time
__ Started a new career
__ Went back to school/college
__ Took personal development course(s)

14. What is your current involvement in volunteer or community organizations? __ Very involved __ Sometimes involved __ Rarely involved __ Not involved at all	17. How would you assess your finances for what you had planned to do after you retired? __ Sufficient to meet my/our needs __ Marginal but sufficient __ Insufficient to meet m/our needs __ Trying to figure this out
15. Did you relocate (move) after retirement? __ Yes to another geographic location __ Yes, to a different home in same city __ Did not relocate or move __ May relocate in the future	18. Do you have hobbies that you enjoy doing? __ Yes, and do on a regular basis __ Yes but rarely do them __ Do not have hobbies

Directions: Check (✓) your response to each of the following statements which that closely describes your feelings **AFTER RETIREMENT**. Use this key:

SA=Strongly Agree **A**=Agree **U**=Undecided
D=Disagree **SA**=Strongly Disagree

STATEMENTS	SA	A	U	D	SD
1. Retirement is what I thought it would be.					
2. I have plenty of things to do that I enjoy.					
3. I enjoy being active.					
4. I feel good about myself.					
5. I have people to rely upon when problems occur.					
6. I enjoy retirement.					
7. I have enough to do with my time.					
8. I get up at the same time as I did before I retired.					
9. Other people say that I am happily retired.					
10. I rarely feel lonely.					
11. A pet is currently an important part of my life.					
12. I have friends that I associate with on a regular basis.					
13. I have sufficient financial resources to meet my basic needs.					
14. People regularly visit my home.					
15. I am rarely bored.					
16. I enjoy life more now that I am retired.					
17. Other people tell me what to do.					
18. My living standards have declined since I retired.					
19. I worry about the future.					
20. I was adequately prepared for retirement.					

21. Depression is a problem for me.					
22. Adjusting to retirement was easy for me.					
23. I worry about my health as I get older.					
24. Retirement is easier for me now than when I first retired.					
IF MARRIED, or HAVE PARTNER					
25. My spouse/partner and I have switched some roles since I retired.					
26. My marriage is more satisfying since I retired.					
27. My spouse/partner and I get along better than we did before I retired.					
28. I sometimes feel in the way around the house.					
29. My spouse/partner and I have better sexual relations than we did before I retired.					
30. My spouse/partner says I am around the house too much.					
31. My spouse/partner and I looked forward to retirement together.					
32. My culture and ethnic background have impacted my retirement.					

Now Think About It

Now that you've done the questionnaire, and discussed it with someone else, think about what you learned. What were the differences in your opinions and those of your family or friends? Did you change your mind about anything after talking with them? Did anyone you talked with changes opinions about anything? If so, what were they? What things do you need to add to your planning? What other persons do you need to include in the planning process? If the other person was your husband, wife, or partner how strongly did you disagree? How did you resolve your conflicts? What plans did you make?

Review the Questions You Answered

As for the questions themselves, there are a number of points to be made. First of all, "How *do you feel* about retirement?" There is a lot involved in the retirement process and a countless changes that will happen. What are your biggest concerns? What do you look forward to the most? Have you really thought about what retirement will be like? As with any transition, a number of other people are also interested in what you will do. Involving them in the process not only makes them feel included, but can prevent problems later on. Many people wait until they retire to figure out what they are going to do with their time, their days, their weeks, and so on. When your life has focused on 40 hours (and more) a week at work and work is removed, you have 40 hours a week, plus travel time, for something else – and it's not always easy to figure out how you are going to use all that newly acquired time.

If your current job is not particularly enjoyable, or even if you hate it, you may be looking forward to retirement. You may have to retire due to your age or company policy. You may just plainly want to quit working. Maybe the job has changed, the boss is no longer someone you want to work with, the work is no longer enjoyable, or you have health problems. Maybe you've been told you have to take an early retirement. Or maybe you were going to be laid off and this forced you to retire. Maybe you've been plunged into retirement without sufficient planning and without sufficient income. Whatever the reasons, you have to evolve into *a retiree -* and that changes your entire life.

> *The question isn't at what age I want to retire, it's at what income.*
> *— George Foreman*

Workers are retiring earlier than ever before and have many productive years ahead. Figuring out what to do with those *years* can be the challenge. Having something to do with your time, and feeling you are needed may be your reasons to return to work. Maybe you don't have enough income. It usually takes retirees longer to find the right job fit, but retail stores and restaurants, in particular, are hiring older workers. These older adults are productive. They show up on time. They are courteous and they enjoy what they are doing. You may want to do something you've always wanted to and just for fun. As the baby boomers retire from one job, many will enter another one. It's also predictable just because they have put in enough years doesn't mean they will retire. Some want to continue so they can maintain their living styles. Others simply enjoy working. People are retiring with sufficiently high incomes and assets to live the same lifestyles they did before they retired. Others are struggling to live comfortably.

Examples to Consider

Russell had been a construction worker in New York his entire working life. After he retired, he moved to a South Carolina beach community and opened a seafood restaurant.

Jack had been retail store owner in Pennsylvania and he retired and opened a children's bookstore in Alabama.

Bill was a retired physician who took up motorcycling and traveled around the country on his Harley.

A nun who had been a teacher all of her life, retired and entered nursing– at 65!

CHAPTER 2

THE IMPORTANCE OF PLANNING

As we said previously, getting ready for retirement includes more than having financial investments, a retirement plan, social security, and a condo with a view. It can be almost a total change in your life - that means how you use your time, when you get up in the morning, what you do with your day, the people you associate with, and what you talk about. Planning for these changes needs careful thought. It includes talking with the other people who share your life, setting new goals for the future – yes the future, and developing realistic, flexible strategies to achieve those goals. It also includes a periodic "self-check" to see where you are, how you are doing, and what additional changes may be needed.

Did You Know?

Only about one-fourth of older adults engage in volunteer activities.

Source: http://www.bls.gov/news.release/volun.nr0.htm

Poor planning can hinder what you've been expecting to do in retirement. Planning for changes in lifestyle and eventually, in health, leads to better retirement adjustment, especially for married couples.

Source: Couture, L. (2011). Planning is key to a healthy and happy retirement. *Activities, Adaptation & Aging, 35*(3), 267-273.

The purpose of planning is to help you prepare for a successful adjustment. You need to acquire skills to move through the transitional period to a new life. Because retirement impacts not only you, but the people around you, discussing your ideas, beliefs, and concerns with others is a part of this planning process. Too often, a husband or wife retires and assumes things are going to be much the same as before retirement - and that everything will work out. Then they find out that their marriage has changed over the years, they don't have as much money as they thought they would, and their likes are different. One or both of the couple's health has declined, the kids live too far away to visit, and the grandkids have grown up. What the couple used to talk about, what they used to do and what they had planned to do after retirement, have all changed significantly. They may even discover that one or both of them just doesn't like retirement! One of the biggest problems occurs when they find out they don't like spending all this time together. In fact, some find out they don't even like each other anymore. The divorce rate for older adults has doubled in recent years and now about one out of every 4 divorces involves an older adult. (http://cleveland.cbslocal.com/2013/07/22/study-divorce-rate-in-older-adults-doubles/#)

I married him for better or for worse, but not for lunch.

When people plan for retirement, they don't think about how they will handle stress, and how their relationships and lives will change. After all, the person you married 50 years ago is not the person you are married to now. Age does matter.

Plan for the best that you want, plan for the worst that can happen, and then plan to be surprised.

Situation

Steve and Lea had been married for over 45 years. Steve had his own real estate business and was quite successful. Before he retired, he sold the business and worked part-time for another agency. About 2 years later, his wife had bypass surgery and a year later had a stroke. She was confined to bed most of the time and needed assistance with all of her care. She had to be carried from one place to another and Steve was her primary caregiver. He needed in-home assistance to help with her care because she could not be left alone. They had been active in social organizations, traveled a great deal, and loved dancing. All of this ended, and abruptly.

Preparing for life after retirement as well as for later life includes taking steps that will promote your own personal health as well as the health of those people who are important to you. If there are very few things that you actually enjoy doing with your time, if you become a "couch potato", if you isolate yourself from other people, then you're pretty likely to find out rather quickly that you're miserable. And if you had few or no outside interests other than work, it may be difficult for you to develop new interests after you're retired. People tend to continue what they have been doing throughout life into their later years.

Of course, it's never too late to get started. Developing things you enjoy and ways to make you feel good about yourself are a part of planning for retirement. Happiness is an integral component of being well adjusted, and vice versa. Contributing to society, doing things you enjoy, having people to rely on when problems arise, and having meaningful relationships enhance the odds that you're going to be happy - and well adjusted.

Planning for retirement can help you prevent isolation, depression, marital problems, and even stress. It can promote a healthy lifestyle and positive thinking which are fundamental in later life. And if you're already retired and having some difficulties, you can start planning, begin making changes to solve some of your problems and prevent future ones. After all, happiness, not work, should now be the focus of your life.

> ***Retirement will finally happen when you realize you have over excelled in work and under excelled in leisure.***

What have you planned so far?

Read the statements listed in the following table. For each item, check (v) how you rate your *current planning* for retirement. If you are already retired, rate how you feel you *actually planned* for retirement. Use this scale:

EP - Excellent Plan   **AP** –Adequate Plan   **NP** - No Plan

Have you thought about *and* planned for...

Questions	EP	AP	NP
1. what you will do to replace work time after retirement?			
2. what you will do with your family after retirement?			
3. how to use your retirement benefits?			
4. adjusting to retirement life?			
5. stress management after retirement?			
6. living with your family after retirement?			
7. your life as you grow even older?			
8. changes in how you spend your days after retirement?			
9. changes in your physical health as you grow older?			
10. relocation after you retire and then in later life?			
11. what your family will do after you retire?			
12. changes in your support system after you are retired?			
13. changes in your support system as you grow older?			
14. what will make you happy after you are retired?			
15. how you will contribute to others when you are retired?			
16. unexpected changes in your plans after you retire?			

Are You Ready to Retire?

This is one of the biggest decisions you have to make in life. It changes nearly every aspect of how you live. So how do you decide when the time is right to retire? Is there a right time? First of all, think about the reasons you *should* and the reasons you *should not* retire. List the other people involved. If you're married, it will impact your spouse or partner, especially if your finances change. What happens when you no longer leave for work in the morning? What if you're stuck spending all this time together? You will suddenly have more time to do volunteer work, play sports, workout or exercise, and even walk the dog. Talk with your family and friends about the changes and what you believe the pros and the cons are for everyone involved. Ask them for their input.

Retirement. Seen it all. Done it all.
Now I get to watch others see it all and do it all.

The Pros Why I <u>Should</u> Retire	The Cons Why I <u>Should</u> <u>Not</u> Retire	Opinions of Others
1.	1.	
2.	2.	
3.	3.	
4.	4.	
5.	5.	
6.	6.	
7.	7.	
8.	8.	

Which list is longer? Can you afford to retire? Do you have the finances to afford what you listed in the Pros column? Is your retirement mandatory?

CHAPTER 3

ROLES & RESPONSIBILITIES: EMPLOYEE RETIREE

"Parts" you play in life are those functions you have, those roles you play in any given situation or group. You may have the role of a spouse, a supervisor, an employee, a parent, the family provider, the support person, a child, the president of an organization, the organist at church or a baseball umpire. People have many roles in life at home, at work and in the community - all at the same time. With retirement there is usually a tremendous change in these roles. Your work roles change the most; but, there are others that change as a result of your retirement. They can also change due to health issues or the health of a family member. Maybe you can no longer mow the lawn or maybe you are now the caretaker of a family member. If you relocate to another area, you will have new roles to play in the community or in your religious group.

Obviously, if you are a company executive and you retire, your role as "the boss" will cease. But some people are surprised to find out that their role in the community can also change. Maybe you are no longer viewed as the influential and powerful "CEO". You're retired. Maybe you enjoy that. Maybe you miss being "the boss". And remember, just because you were the boss at work, doesn't mean you can suddenly become the boss at home to replace that role. Identifying the roles you have while working, and then the roles you will have after retirement are essential in figuring out what changes you will need to adjust to. Identifying which roles you will miss is equally important in finding new ones that will meet your needs and provide you with things you really enjoy.

Directions: Fill in your responses in the following table. If you are **NOT RETIRED**, list your **current roles**. If you **ARE RETIRED**, list the **roles you had before retirement**.

There are some examples to get you started.

Work Roles

List 10 Roles You Now Have <u>at Work</u> OR You Had When Working	If You Are <u>NOT RETIRED</u> Check (√) Those Roles Which Will Change When You Retire	If You <u>ARE RETIRED</u> Check (√) Those Roles Which Changed When You Retired
1. Supervisor	1.	1.
2. Boss	2.	2.
3 Budget Manager	3.	3.
4. Teacher	4.	4.
5.	5.	5.
6.	6.	6.
7.	7.	7.
8.	8.	8.
9.	9	9.
10.	10.	10.

Home & Family Roles

List 10 Roles You Now Have at Home OR Had When Working	If You Are NOT RETIRED Check (√) Those Roles Which Will Change When You Retire	If You ARE RETIRED Check (√) Those Roles Which Changed When You Retired
1. Cook	1.	1.
2. Gardener	2.	2.
3. Income Provider	3.	3.
4. Repairman	4.	4.
5.	5.	5.
6.	6.	6.
7.	7.	7.
8.	8.	8.
9.	9.	9.
10.	10.	10.

Community Roles

List 10 Roles You Now Have **In Your Community** OR Had When Working	If You Are **NOT RETIRED** Check (√) Those Roles Which Will Change When You Retire	If You **ARE RETIRED** Check (√) Those Roles Which Changed When You Retired
1. Little League Coach	1.	1.
2. Civic Board Member	2.	2.
3. Religious Teacher	3.	3.
4. Fund Raiser	4.	4.
5.	5.	5.
6.	6.	6.
7.	7.	7.
8.	8.	8.
9.	9.	9.
10.	10	10.

Other Roles

List Any <u>Other Roles</u> You Now Have <u>OR</u> You Had When Working	If You Are <u>NOT RETIRED</u> Check (√) Those Roles Which Will Change When You Retire	If You <u>ARE RETIRED</u> Check (√) Those Roles Which Changed When You Retired
1. State Legislator	1.	1.
2. Task Force Chair	2.	2.
3.	3.	3.
4.	4.	4.
5.	5.	5.

Changes in Your Roles

Who Expects What of You?

Whether at work, at home, or in the community, you have roles and you know what they involve. But remember, sometimes what *you* think your roles are, and what *other* people think they are, just might not match. You are the supervisor of 10 employees, the budget manager, the primary income provider, a Little League Coach. You consider yourself a role model as an employee and a professional at what you do. You may expect yourself to be the best boss in the company or the person who gets the most new contracts. Others also have expectations of you. As an employee, you may be *"expected"* to attend the annual company picnic, meet deadlines, contribute to the holiday giving fund, and call your office once a day when you are out of town on business, while checking your e-mail! Whatever the expectations, when you reach them, or even when you sort of reach them, you get a sense of satisfaction and perhaps even status within the business or wherever you work. This contributes to how positively you feel about yourself. The expectations of you come from the expectations of your bosses as well as from the overall values, mission, and policies of the organization. They also come from within you as a result of your work ethic, and your career goals. Some of these expectations probably created problems for you, but they were there. Retirement brings these job expectations, these employment roles to a halt. It also cuts off both the positive, and negative, feelings and rewards you got from them.

Listen to what others expect of you.

When you're working, your family sees you in certain roles, both at work and at home. Being an electrician or a secretary, or a vice-president gives you some degree of recognition in your family and in the community. You may be looked to for leadership in a civic organization, or for being a leader in the Scouts, not only due to the contributions you can make, but because of your position at work and the status you bring to the organization or team. People associate you with a particular agency or business. Your friends know where you work and may even be aware of special challenges, problems, and recognitions you have had. You not only provide financial income, but you may also provide some sort of social distinction.

When you meet somebody new, you nearly always get the question, "What do you do?" or "Where do you work?" It's a social introduction. You answer by saying where you work and what kind of job you have. Or you say you are a stay-at-home wife or husband. This doesn't really say who you are, but it is an expectation in our society as a kind of greeting. Your friends and family already know what you do. *"Did your wife get that promotion?" "My brother works with your son in the XYZ company. How's it going over there?"* Then, *"Where did you go to school or college?"* is almost as instantaneous and common as *"How are you?"* It is a way of getting to know more about you and getting a superficial conversation started. From that point on, you are associated with a work setting, an employer and the profession or craft that you are in. The next time you meet, the conversation may even start from there.

There are a number of issues that you should think about. This will help you get a better idea of how things change with retirement and what you may want to do about addressing those changes. In the following section, ask yourself all of the questions that are listed. If you are planning to retire, there is one set of questions. If you are already retired there is another set. Think. And be honest. After you're done, once again set up a time to discuss everything with someone you trust and is special to you. Whose expectations are you going to meet?

I am not in this world to live up to other people's expectations, nor do I feel that the world must live up to mine." Fritz Peris

Role Expectations. Questions to Ask Yourself

Planning for Retirement	Already Retired
1. What are the 5 biggest expectations of you in your work role? Who expects them?	1. What 5 changes have occurred in your roles since you retired? How have these changes impacted you?
1.	1.
2.	2.
3.	3.
4.	4.
5.	5.
2. What kind of status does your work give you?	2. What kind of status did work give you that you no longer have?
3. What kind of status does your work give other people important to you?	3. What status did your work role give other people important to you?

4. What impact will retirement have on what you expect of yourself?	4. What impact did retirement have on what you expect of yourself?
5. What impact will retirement have on what others expect of you?	5. What impact did retirement have on what others expect of you?
6. How will retirement change your status in your family? in your community?	6. How did retirement change your status in your family? in your community?
7. What responsibilities will you miss after retirement?	7. What responsibilities do you miss since you retired?

Planning for Changes in Roles

Planning for Retirement	Already Retired
1. Identify 5 new roles you would like to have in your family after you retire? 1. 2, 3, 4. 5.	1. Identify 5 new roles you have or would like to have in your family since you retired. 1. 2. 3. 4. 5.
2. List 5 things about your job that you feel gives you status in your family or community. 1. 2. 3. 4. 5.	2. List 5 roles you have or would like to have in your community that give you status.

3. Identify 5 new roles you would like to have in your community after you retire.	3. Identify 5 new roles you have or would like to have in your community since you retired.
3. Discuss with family members what you would like to be involved in after you retire. Identify things that will mean you are making a meaningful contribution. Identify things you can do with family members.	3. Discuss with family members what you would like to be involved in now that you are retired. Identify things that mean you are making a meaningful contribution. Identify things you can do with family members.

Some Jargon – Role Ambiguity, Role Reversal, and Role Conflict

With retirement comes a time to look not only at your roles, but the roles of those significant other people in your life. Among married couples, for instance, it is not uncommon to have some role reversal. For example, both the husband and wife may decide to retire at the same time or nearly so. If the husband has retired, he may assume more household duties at home such as cooking meals, cleaning the house, and doing laundry. The wife may get a job *"on the outside"* - either full-time or part-time, even if she was not previously employed. She might take over yard chores. In years past, it was primarily the husband who retired because many wives did not work outside the home. Now, there are many marriages where both of the couples are employed and have been so for many years. It could be the wife who retires first. In any case, role reversal can still occur.

When two people switch roles it is sometimes due to necessity, but it may also be because the person who's now at home wants to be needed and have something to do. This in itself can cause conflict - unless there are discussions about what roles will be assumed and by whom. Having to take on new responsibilities for which you were not prepared can create its own set of tensions. In addition, if you don't carry out these new duties the way others expect you to – the way they would have done them – there can be conflict. *"You didn't put the dishes on the right shelf." "The underwear doesn't go in that drawer." "The lawn is mowed too short." "What happened to the screwdriver that was in the toolbox?"* Roles become unclear. Roles are in conflict, and stress results.

When somebody just takes over what another person has been doing, both role ambiguity and role conflict can result. For the single person, this ambiguity may be more evident in roles with friends, or in organizations in the community. Some retirees start taking over control in social organizations – in opposition to what the membership wants. This can happen when the loss of being in charge at work creates a vacuum that needs to be filled, but it also creates conflict, and even enemies!

In couples, some of the role confusion can result from simply having too much free time, or being around the house more. This doesn't say, however, that all changes, including role reversal are necessarily negative. There may be those roles that you want to give up, like doing the grocery shopping or taking the clothes to the dry cleaner. But this requires negotiation and everyone agreeing on the changes – before they occur. Surprises are not always welcome when it comes to doing the household chores.

What about the expectations from your kids? Do you really want to be the built-in baby sitter? You may enjoy the grandkids, but you will have to work out how much time you are going to devote to them and how this will impact *your* use of time. Just because you're now retired your children or even grandchildren, may decide that you are a free source of babysitting for their kids. You may enjoy watching over them, or even the neighbor kids who come to get cookies on Saturday afternoons. But it should be *your* decision, and put into your schedule because that's what *you* want. Does your own cultural background, your heritage, have an impact on expectations of you in your family and community?

> *I'm not a role model... Just because I dunk a basketball doesn't mean I should raise your kids. Charles Barkley*

Situation:

> Sarah and Dennis have been married for many years. Dennis retired four months ago and has been staying around the house a lot. Sarah complains that she can't get her housework done because Dennis sleeps until 8 am. When he gets up, he immediately asks *"What's for breakfast?"* Then it's *"What's for lunch?"*. By mid-afternoon he is asking *"How will you fix the roast I brought home for dinner?"* Sarah says he constantly *"meddles"* in all the housework and tells her how to do everything. He spends the rest of the day watching TV or playing on the computer. He's taken over all the family planning based on what *he* wants both of them to do, and when they should do it.

Not only is this a problem for Sarah and how she wants to use her time, but before Dennis retired, Sarah didn't even eat lunch! Now she is constantly preparing meals, while trying to complete her normal household duties around his sleeping and TV patterns. Dennis expects a full lunch AND he expects Sarah to eat with him. She has tried to put up with his wishes (rather than discussing the problem) and is upset that she's already gained 14 pounds since *he* retired. This situation clearly needs some work. She is expected to assume the role of cook and rearrange her day to meet the expectations of Dennis. Communication just isn't happening. Dennis is having trouble adjusting and needs to focus on his own roles and the use of his own time. He's changed his *"work hours"* into *"bored hours"*. Neither one of them is facing the problem. There is confusion regarding expectations, and there is growing conflict. And Dennis has too much spare time! It's important for the retiree and significant others to examine which roles they want to change and which are meaningful to each, as well as need to be fulfilled by the right person. Respect for the other person's time is essential.

Changes in Roles - Questions to Ask Yourself

Planning for Retirement	Already Retired
1. How will my roles in my family change when I retire?	1. How have my roles in my family changed since I retired?
2. What are the roles in my family that someone else has that I will or want to assume?	2. What roles have I assumed since I retired that someone else had before I retired?
3. Does the other person want to give up the roles that I want to assume?	3. Did the other person want to give up the roles that I assumed from him or her?

4. Who should I talk with about these changes in roles?	4. Did I talk with the person whose roles I assumed about these changes? If not, should I do so now or was it necessary?
5. What will be my new roles?	5. What are my new roles since I retired?
6. What conflicts do I foresee with any changes in my roles?	6. What conflicts have occurred over changing my roles?

Strategies for Adjusting to Changes in Your Roles

Planning for Retirement	Already Retired
1. Talk with family and friends about what retirement means to you.	1. Talk with family and friends about what retirement has meant to you.
2. Talk with family and friends about how your roles are going to change when you retire.	2. Talk with family and friends about how your roles have changed since you retired.
3. Discuss which of your roles will change with retirement.	3. Discuss role changes with the other people involved if possible.
4. Identify people with whom you may have conflicts over roles and discuss the issues with them.	4. Identify people with whom you may have conflicts over roles and discuss the issues with them.
5. Talk with other retirees.	5. Talk with other retirees.

Role Stress

Having a job usually includes role *"stressors"* that come from the normal pressures and responsibilities of the workplace, as well as the occasional crisis. You have pressures from the boss, the budget or financial issues, temperamental clients or personnel problems – and you have to handle them. It is your job, your role to do so. Most people develop coping mechanisms and strategies to deal with them and mechanisms to solve the problems. If not, you stay stressed and have to tolerate the situations – or quit. The stressors vary with the position, the events, the situations, people you work with, and who you are as an employee. But...they stop completely after you retire.

Deadlines aren't so important, until they have passed.

You no longer have the work role, the boss, the employees, the budget, the cranky client, or the time clock. This is what many employees look forward to and what retirees enjoy. Retirement is a time to be free of work responsibilities and the opportunity to move on in life. And yet, many are not prepared for the reality of having all this *"free of stress time"* available to them.

Did You Know?

Retirement may be seen by women as a time to take back their lives and control what's going on.

Source: Seaman, P. (2012). Taking back my life. Early boomer women's anticipation of retirement and volunteering. *Dissertation Abstracts International Section A: Humanities and Social Sciences, 72*(8-A). 2663.

With retirement, new stressors can arise - in the home, the family, or the community. Perhaps you have an unemployed adult child and two kids who move in with you. Maybe you have an elderly parent who needs constant supervision or care. You may be the chair of a community organization that is in financial trouble, or you may be having financial problems yourself. The coping mechanisms you used in the work setting may or may not work in these situations. You may need to rely on what worked for you in the past with your family or friends. How did you handle the stresses at work? How did you cope? When did you relax? What helped you do that? You may also have to develop new ways to cope – ways you have not had to know before. You may need to find someone to help care for an aging parent at night. You may need to set limits on the adult child with kids who moved in, and establish who the actual parent is. Perhaps the kids need to be responsible for doing the dishes, their own laundry, mowing the lawn every Saturday. If you are on a fixed income for the first time, and that income is substantially less than what you had when you are working, you will need a new approach to finances, budgets, and certainly your expenses. These things can all be stressors...!

Did You Know?

Retirement may not always be stressful. Some people consider the role transition a self-actualizing event and increases their sense of well-being. It can be an energizing and fulfilling experience.

Source: Fehr, R. (2012). Is retirement always stressful? The potential impact of creativity. *American Psychologist, 67*(1), 76-77.

As a result of financial stresses and strains, many retirees return to work. Some find this annoying or even degrading but feel they have to supplement their income. You may not like having to get a part-time job just because your retirement income is not sufficient to maintain your living standards. With the recent decline in the stock market, many retirees are finding that they have less income than they thought they would have. If you were forced into an early retirement or retired because of health reasons you may have additional financial burdens. Hence, you may have less money to do the things you planned for retirement. You may not be able to afford the type of housing, level of living, or those "extras" that you had counted on. Former travel plans may no longer be realistic.

Being retired can be stressful for those people who don't feel productive, who don't feel useful, have too much time on their hands, or *"feel in the way around the house"*. You may enjoy having your husband or wife at home all the time. But if you have been accustomed to having either of you at work five days a week while you spent the days doing what you wanted to, you may feel like kicking somebody out of the house once in a while.

For fast-acting relief, try slowing down. Lily Tomlin

Situation

George and Jean had been married for a little over 25 years. George retired as the CEO of a major company. They bought a new home and moved south. George began doing some part-time consulting for a small new business, but it was only for a few hours a week. Jean was perfectly content to stay at home, decorate her new home, and was beginning to join social groups. She spent a great deal of time organizing the kitchen, getting the furniture where she wanted it and doing some decorating. Sam showed no interest at all in any of these activities.

Very quickly, George began to get bored. He tried golf, but didn't really like it and besides he didn't know people to play with him. He soon lost interest. Jean met a group of friends at one of the organizations she joined and they started meeting every Wednesday for lunch. She would have her hair done and then join them at the same restaurant each week. On one of the Wednesdays that she was out, George got bored and decided to re-organize the kitchen – in *alphabetical order*, cups to saucers. Everything was in a *logical order*, according to him. He made little stickers to go on the edge of the shelves, put the spices allspice to paprika, and generally did a major overhaul.

Jean came home and *"exploded"*. *"What the Hell did you do? I just spent six weeks getting all this organized. You don't even cook and you're never in the kitchen anyway."* George couldn't understand her reaction, but obviously *management by objectives* was definitely not going over well in the kitchen!

Role Stress - Questions to Ask Yourself

Planning for Retirement	Already Retired
1. What stressors do you foresee in your role as a retiree?	1. What stressors do you feel in your role as a retiree?
2. With whom have you discussed what you foresee as stressors as a retiree?	2. With whom have you discussed those things that cause you stress as a retiree?
3. What roles will you have to assume that someone else currently does that will give you stress?	3. What roles have you assumed that someone else used to do that now give you stress?

4. What can you do now to prevent some of the stress in your roles as a retiree?	4. What things could you change if you were able to that would decrease your current stress?
5. Do you understand what stresses you may have after you retire?	5. What can be done to reduce your stress? Who can help with this?
6. What do other people say is going to cause you stress?	6. What do other people say is causing you stress?
7. What do you do to relieve stress? What works the best? What new skills to reduce stress do you need to learn?	7. What do you do to relieve stress? What works the best? What new skills to reduce stress do you need to learn?

Strategies to Cope With Stress

Planning for Retirement	Already Retired
1. Identify things that cause you stress when you are working and how these may get better or worse after retirement.	1. Identify what things cause you the most stress in retirement.
2. Talk with someone else about stress reduction strategies	2. Talk with someone else about stress reduction strategies.
3. Develop strategies to reduce any stress you are feeling or may feel after retirement. Go to the list of Stress Reduction Strategies in the Appendix Select three (3) that you are going to try. Develop a schedule for doing stress reduction. After one week and one month, evaluate how they are or are not helping you. List them here:	3. Develop strategies to reduce any stress you are feeling. Go to the list of Stress Reduction Strategies in the Appendix Select three (3) that you are going to try. Develop a schedule for doing stress reduction. After one week and one month, evaluate how they are or are not helping you. List them here:

4. If you don't have one, develop an exercise schedule appropriate for you. Be certain that it has the clearance of your physician if needed.	4. If you don't have one, develop an exercise schedule appropriate for you. Be certain that it has the clearance of your physician if needed.
5. Practice stress reduction strategies at least once a day.	5. Practice stress reduction strategies at least once a day.
6. Talk with retirees about what they do to reduce their stress.	6. Talk with other retirees about what they do to reduce their stress.

Role Maintenance – Keeping Some Roles

Not all roles stop after retirement. It's important to keep those that *can reasonably be assumed* to be workable and rewarding. Involvement in the home, the family, and the community can be sources of enjoyment and contribute to your sense of well-being. Maintaining roles that are meaningful, constructive, and provide a contribution to others is one of the ways in which retirees *continue* to be productive members of society. Retirement is a new way of life, not the end of the road.

There are many professional roles that can actually be maintained after retirement, but in a slightly different form. If you were a university professor, you can still write, publish, and do research. If you were a physical therapist, you can work part-time. If you were a construction worker, you can take part-time jobs, or serve as a consultant. If you were a business executive, you can assist small businesses. Perhaps you owned your own business, and can now assist young entrepreneurs. If you were a medical transcriptionist, you can work part-time in a physician's office or online. These not only provide income, but allow you to share your expertise with less experienced, younger workers. It gives them the benefit of your knowledge and skills while giving you extra income and a sense of being able to continue to contribute to your profession or craft. Working part-time can be one way to phase in retirement without giving up all of your work interests. Just be careful which roles you pick and make certain that you really are able to do them. Climbing on roofs, landscaping yards, painting houses, chopping down trees, or chasing 30 toddlers around a day care center all day may not be your smartest choices…!

Situation

> Marybeth retired a few months ago as the Vice-President of Human Resources for a large hospital. She and a small group of other retirees get together a couple of times a month for dinner just to maintain their ties and socialize. One of the group members, Robert, is married to another HR staff member who is still at the hospital. Marybeth spends much of the group's time telling her retired colleagues how the hospital should be run. She also puts considerable pressure on Robert to tell his wife how to handle personnel matters, which policies should be changed, and which employees she thinks are creating problems for the hospital. Her friends are getting tired of her nagging and *"meddling"* in hospital business.

Marybeth no longer works at the hospital, and but she continues to try to influence decisions. This suggests that she hasn't really cut the ties and adjusted to retirement. She needs to look at what she is doing, and the impact her behavior is having on others, as well as on herself. She could profit from some outlets for her energies that are more constructive and channeled in a different direction. There may be a community organization where she could use some of her skills *without* trying to continue running the affairs of the hospital where she once worked. If she doesn't change her intrusive behavior, she will probably find out rather quickly that the group won't include her any longer. In situations like this, if she doesn't cut the ties, the group will probably do it for her. They may also just tell her to *"butt out"*.

In order to have roles that can be maintained *after* retirement, they usually have to be developed *before* retirement. One part of preparation for retirement is to develop interests and activities that are not linked to the job. This might include social activities, involvement in religious organizations, new hobbies, volunteering at a shelter, and today - the use of technology! Computers are an excellent way to stay in touch with other people, learn new information, and use your time constructively.

If you are involved in organizations, cultural events, educational programs, politics, *before* you retire, you can continue this involvement *after* you retire. You may also decide to try a new career, or go back to school. If so, begin to plan for this before you retire. Check out jobs sites and see what interests you. What is the pay scale? How many hours would you have to work? Are the hours flexible? Do they hire someone with your particular set of skills? Check out what courses are being taught at your local college or university. Consider continuing education and low cost short courses as well. Many courses are now available on the Internet. You don't even have to travel to get enrolled or complete the course. It also might expose you to younger students in the class where you can learn about their beliefs and what's going on in *their* world. If you have the money, consider a group travel tour or an educational cruise.

Involvement in activities that are physical, mental, spiritual and social are essential to a well-rounded individual. There needs to be a balance and a commitment to self-fulfillment in later life. The more options there are before retirement, the more likelihood at least some can be pursued after retirement.

Role Maintenance - Questions to Ask Yourself

Planning for Retirement	Already Retired
1. Which of your current roles can you reasonably expect to continue after you retire? List.	1. Which of my current roles did you have before you retired? List.
2. Which of your current roles will cease after you retire? List.	2. Which of my current roles do you value the most? the least? List.
3. Of the roles that will cease, which will you miss the most? the least? List.	3. What new roles do you want to have? List.

4. What new roles do you want to have after you retire? List.	4. What roles do you see for yourself in the future that you don't currently have?
5. How will you go about setting up these new roles before you retire?	5. How can you go about setting up the new roles that you want?
6. What resources do you need and who do you need to contact?	6. What resources are available to you?

Strategies for Keeping Some of Your Roles

Planning for Retirement	Already Retired
1. Talk with family and friends about how you see yourself in retirement. Ask for their suggestions. List.	1. .Talk with family and friends about how you see yourself in retirement. Ask for their suggestions. List.
2. Consider which work roles can be developed in different ways. Examples: If you are a business person, consider being a consultant, consider working part-time, etc. Comments:	2. Consider any of the roles that you had when you were working that could be used in different ways now. Comments:
3. Consider how you can use your talents and skills in your community with organizations, the church, or in political settings. Comments:	3. Consider how you can use your talents and skills in your community with organizations, the church, or in political settings.
4. List the new things you want to do and begin working on them *before* you retire so that they are in place *after* you retire. List.	4. Talk with family members and friends about what new roles you might assume.
5. List activities that demonstrate to you and others that you are contributing something meaningful to other people and society.	5. Talk with other retirees about what is working for them.

Role Transition – Moving On

Whether retirement is your own choice, or whether it's "*forced*" upon you by virtue of your age or policies, it is a major life transition. Going from working with all of the structure, responsibilities, and obligations to total free time requires an adjustment. Some people find it easy – a relief! Others have more difficulty. First you have to make the decision to retire, then decide on a date and make that date known. You may also reduce your hours and work part-time at your current job for a while. This eases you into the retirement role. A part of the process is including other people in your decisions, looking at the various alternatives, and making concrete plans. Look at the choices and alternatives that you have. Involve others as you think about it.

Did You Know?

- 39% of women and 20% of men expect to live to age 90 or more.

- **Source**: MetLife Mature Market Institute. https://www.metlife.com/mmi/research/women-retirement-extra-long-life.html#findings

---

"When do I make it official?" "How do I want to leave?" Some people want a party and make it a major event, while others want to leave without ceremony. Others have no choice because it's decided by the company. Some professions have a mandatory retirement age to ensure the safety of the consumer public. Determining what's involved in your actual retirement *"event"* - and then deciding what to do immediately afterwards can help to ease the transition. What would you like to have happen? Talk with friends and people who are already retired as well as people who are getting ready to retire. Then, talk with the people in human resources where you work. Find out about your retirement benefits. Keep in mind that companies and unions continue to cut retirement benefits. Estimate what your income will be from your pension plan as well as any other sources of income that you have. Fill out the necessary forms. Learn about social security, Medicare, and any health insurance from where you have been working. Locate the Social Security office and visit it. There is a lot of paper work to do and it must be done early. Applications can be filled out

online and the rules about age requirements and when to apply are clearly laid out in the instructions. Check with an accountant about your income tax and how much money you can make before paying taxes in case you decide to get another job. Make out a calendar of events to address the many deadlines involved.

This book is not designed to help you with the financial aspects of retirement. There are a lot of books in libraries, online and in bookstores to help you with all of those details. Many are well worth reading. Visit some of the major book retailers on the Internet. Determine your net worth and what your income will be. List the amount and sources of actual cash. Make a list of your investments, the market value of any real estate you own, and the value of personal property. Develop a realistic budget. Determine your expenses for a month and for a year, noting that some expenses only occur once a year. Then compare your income with your proposed expenses. Include the cost of running your home, such as electricity and utilities. Add transportation or travel expenses, entertainment and hobbies, food and eating out, health care costs, veterinary bills, and clothing expenses. Having a budget that will work for you is essential in the transition in order to avoid having greater needs than you have income to meet. And obviously, this planning begins long before retirement. But again, it's not too late to start.

Making the Retirement Decision

Planning for Retirement	Already Retired
1. Who will decide on your retirement date? your or someone else?	1. Was retirement your choice or was it imposed by the company or agency?
2. Is retirement your choice or is it being imposed by the company or agency?	2. What do you like about your decision to retire, if it was your choice?
3. What do you need to consider about retiring?	3. What do you dislike about your decision to retire, if it was your choice?
4. What do you expect from the company when you leave? What will the company provide to show you have retired?	4. How did the company handle your retirement? How do you feel about the way the company handled your retirement?
5. What do you want to do to celebrate or announce your retirement?	5. Are you well informed on your retirement benefits? If not, how do you find out more?
6. What do you need to know about retirement benefits and policies? Who do you ask? What resources do you need and where do you find them?	6. Has anything changed regarding what you expected and what actually happened with regard to your benefits?
7. Do you have a budget? Do I know your net worth and expected expenses following retirement?	7. Do you have a budget? Do I know your net worth and expected expenses following retirement?

Planning the Retirement Event

Planning for Retirement	Already Retired
1. Read the company or agency policies on retirement.	Note: strategies will vary with the length of time since you retired. 1. Determine if any company policies have changed since you retired that effect you personally.
2. Decide on a date to retire.	2. Identify any areas that you are still having trouble adjusting to and then think about what you can do to change anything.
3. Determine how you want your retirement handled. Do you want a celebration? Who do you want to include?	3. Establish a calendar of what you plan to do. a. during the next week? b. during the next month? c. within in six months?
4. Determine who you should be talking with about your decision to retire. Then include them in your decision-making.	4. Establish some personal goals. a. for the next six months? b. for the next year? c. for the next five years?
5. Determine when you will notify the company or agency of your plans to retire. Check with the policies.	5. Are you happy about the way you retired? a. yes b. no
6. Make a calendar for what you plan to do following retirement. a. the week after retirement. b. the month after retirement. c. the year after retirement. (Develop a calendar of events.)	6. Make a calendar for what you plan to do during retirement. a. the week after retirement. b. the month after retirement. c. the year after retirement. (Develop a calendar of events.)
7. Set priorities for what you want to do. a. the most desirable b. acceptable c. the least desirable	7. Set priorities for what you want to do. a. the most desirable b. acceptable c. the least desirable
8. Set some personal goals for: a. six months after retirement b. one year after retirement c. five years after retirement?	8. Set some personal goals for: a. the next six months b. for the next year
9. Develop a budget. Itemize your net worth and your proposed expenses following retirement.	9. Develop a budget. Itemize your net worth and your proposed expenses following retirement.

First Week Calendar of "To Do's"

Activity Code: 1=Must or Need to Do   2=Would Like to Do   3=Can Live Without But...

	SUN	MON	TUE	WED	THU	FRI	SAT
AM	1 2 3	1 2 3	1 2 3	1 2 3	1 2 3	1 2 3	1 2 3
PM	1 2 3	1 2 3	1 2 3	1 2 3	1 2 3	1 2 3	1 2 3

First Month Calendar of "To Do's"

Activity Code: 1=Must or Need to Do   2=Would Like to Do   3=Can Live Without But...

SUN	MON	TUE	WED	THU	FRI	SAT
			1	1		

First Year Calendar of "To Do's"

Activity Code: 1=Must or Need to Do   2=Would Like to Do   3=Can Live Without But…

January	February	March	April	May
June	July	August	September	October
November	December			

First Five Year Calendar of "To Do's"

Activity Code: 1=Must or Need to Do   2=Would Like to Do   3=Can Live Without But...

	Spring	Summer	Fall	Winter
Year One				
Year Two				
Year Three				
Year Four				
Year Five				

CHAPTER 4

CHANGING RELATIONSHIPS

People to People Changes

When moving from a job to retirement, there will be major changes in who you associate with. Former co-workers will most likely no longer be your primary contacts. In fact, ties may actually be severed completely with the majority of the people you work with, unless you switch to part-time first. Although you might have an *"alumni"* organization or agree informally that you will continue to see some of these friends. This sometimes happens with retired military, university faculty, company employees and school teachers. Yet, in retirement, people frequently lose contact with former employers and co-workers over time. Retirees move on to a new set of relationships and relocate older ones. The reasons are quite simple. You may no longer live in the same geographic location. You no longer have the same things in common. Complaints about the *"boss"*, the budget, lack of working equipment, computer crashes, not enough vacation time – are no longer the focus for you when you retire. And let's face it, former co-workers have difficulty relating to someone who goes for a swim every morning, travels, prunes roses, plays golf and makes pottery...! Other retirees just decide to cut all ties with their former workplace and move on to a new life. They just don't want to stay in touch with the people they once worked with.

Jason was a university faculty member who retired after 30 years of teaching.

He had been actively involved in research, had numerous doctoral students, grants, and many publications. When he retired, he became very active in his church and cut off all ties with former colleagues at the university. If someone called him, he would chat politely, but never initiated any contacts himself. He established a new life, and one that was totally separate from his university career.

In one community of note, every Wednesday morning the retirees from the local telephone company meet at a local diner for breakfast. But now they have something new in common – retirement. They talk about what they are doing, the local events, the news, family illnesses. This has been going on for many, many years. When members of the group move away or die, other newer members join. When one member of the group has problems, the others rally around with support. They have continued to be a tightly knit group and meet, no matter the weather or crises. The focus of these gatherings is no longer work. It's their daily personal lives. They talk about what's important to them now…and their friendships.

Life gives you a second chance, every day. It's called tomorrow.

In a local retirement community, there is a group of men who are primarily in their 80s and are friends within that community. Every Tuesday morning they meet in the club room for coffee. Their discussions focus on whatever is going on in the community, local and national politics, the books they have read, and upcoming travels. They are a very affluent, well-educated bunch of gentlemen who not only have a lot in common, but a lot to talk about it. And much of it is about their lives –with a great sense of humor. There is no complaining about their aches and pains – not allowed – because everybody has the same ones. It's about living, being productive, and enjoying one another's company. PS – it's a guys only group…!!!

Humor is one of the foundations of life. Being able to laugh and enjoy the many changes can contribute positively to your ability to cope with situations. Laughter is a diversion from stressors and it nourishes the soul.

> ### *You know your life is boring*
> ### *if you don't know what you laugh at, or when.*

Situation

Ralph really hated going to weddings, and lately it seemed like all of his friends' grandkids were getting married – and he was expected to attend. He met one of those friends, Jim, in the grocery store one Saturday. Jim asked him if he would be at his granddaughter's wedding the following Sunday. Ralph said, *"No, I'm going to a funeral."* Jim said, *"Oh, I'm sorry. Who died?"* Ralph calmly replied, *"I don't know yet"*…!!!

> ### *Even if you are on the right track, you'll get run*
> ### *over if you just sit there. Will Rogers*

A part of the transition to retirement is assessing relationships and figuring out the ones that will change and the ones that will remain intact. It's a time to establish new ones and make new friends; it's a time to re-establish contact with former friends and relatives that you haven't seen for a while. But it doesn't mean visiting all of them to get free room and board for a vacation…! They may not even want you to see you. Remember, they have their own lives too. If you're going to visit, make sure the visits are reciprocal, and agreed on well in advance. Be prepared to share expenses, including helping with the cost of meals. If you go out to dinner, pay your own way. Some guests unfortunately expect to be guests for dinner, too. *"Moochers"* are rarely the basis of long term friendships.

Making the retirement transition is considerably less problematic when you have already made friendships *prior* to retirement. It means making an effort to figure out who you want your friends to be and what family members you want included in your post- retirement life. One of the long term strategies for success is to have a variety of different types of friends, close and not-so-close relationships, different age groups, and ones in social outlets. Many should have nothing to do with work. Don't wait until you retire to figure out who your friends really are! Some will continue after retirement. They provide not only continuity in your life, but a sense of meaningful stability over time. Think about your friends and family. What age groups do they include? Do you socialize with younger people? Older people? Where do they live? How often do you see them? Do you connect by email or texting? Are you on any of the social media sites? Who would you like to be around that you currently do not see? Who do the people you live with want to see? What friends and family do you have in common? Who do you NOT want to see?

Not all relationships endure time...nor should they.

Situation

When Beth and Mark were in their mid-50s they bought a vacant lot in a retirement community in the western US. A few years later, they built a new house there for their retirement. At age 62 Mark had a heart attack and died. Two years later Beth retired and moved to their new house – alone. She quickly learned that everyone else in the neighborhood was married and she was not fitting in, nor was she being very well accepted. She was never invited to social functions. She no longer had a golf partner and had to go to dinner and outings alone. Her task now was either to relocate again or find ways of establishing a circle of friends and a support system.

She joined a church that had an older singles group and became involved. Shortly thereafter, she got involved in two civic organizations. Her life quickly began to change. Although her husband was not alive, she had managed to begin her own new life in retirement. Her church group provided some stability and a new support system. The social groups gave her contacts and time to interact with younger people that were not in her age group. She soon became more accepted as a single person within the groups, and much happier in her new home.

Religious Beliefs

What about religion? Is this something important to you? Your relationships involve a lot more than just the people you associate with. The spiritual relationships that you have can be even more important, and for some people, become increasingly so as they age and start thinking about the end of their lives. It's a time to look back, reminisce, a time for reflection, *and* a time to think about the future. Spirituality can take many forms and you need to decide what's important to you. How are you going to fulfill your own inner needs? Are you active in any religious groups - a church, synagogue, temple, or other place? Do you have religious statutes, icons, pictures, books, in your home? Do you participate in religious services? Are members of your family or friends included? Do your religious connections promote social and spiritual activities? How do your spiritual beliefs impact your beliefs, values, and perceptions of your world? How do you contribute to others based on those beliefs? How do they impact your planning for the future?

Relationships with Pets

Another type of relationship for many people includes having a pet. Whether this is the family dog, a cat, a horse, a bird or some other creature, it is often a way to have a meaningful, loving, living being that you can care for and that will love you back - unconditionally. This can be especially important for people who live alone. But you have to like pets, and they have to be allowed where you live. The latter is much less of a problem than it used to be. Caring for a dog or cat can take money for food and grooming, time, and yes - those expensive vet bills. Make sure you can afford one and have the transportation to get you and your pet to the vet to keep immunizations and exams up to date. The research is very clear. A pet can decrease loneliness, lower blood pressure, promote physical activity, increase longevity and help prevent depression and isolation, while giving you companionship and the opportunity to be a caregiver. Not everyone wants, can, or should have a pet. Yet, the relationship between a pet and its caregiver can be even more meaningful than the relationship between the caregiver and the humans. Unfortunately there are people who have pets who can't care for them adequately and can't afford them.

"*Whiskers*" doesn't care if you have arthritis, gray hair, or even if you're grumpy! He will be there to get you up in the morning and provide you companionship. Having a pet does mean, however, that you have the additional responsibility of caring for another being. This impacts your travel plans, visiting friends and relatives, having them visit you, and what you do with the pet if you need to leave town unexpectedly. Internet sites now exist where you can find which hotels and motels allow pets. Some may require a deposit or an additional fee, so ask in advance when you make your reservations. Many retirees decide a pet is no longer for them because of the many constraints and responsibilities.

Just make sure to plan for the care of your pet if you become ill and when you die. The animal does not need to suffer or be put in a shelter because you are not there to care for it. And remember, particularly as you age, the loss of a beloved pet can be more traumatic and more enduring than the loss of a human family member.

The many relationships you have can influence how you feel about yourself, can impact your own self-esteem, and certainly how you use your time and structure your days. Isolation begets isolation. Loneliness begets loneliness. Having contact with "*meaningful others*" is an important part of feeling needed and contributing to society. Relationships require mutual understanding, reciprocity, and the exchange of feelings, beliefs and new ideas.

There are a variety of sources of relationships. They come from family, friends, organizations, church groups, people you met on a trip or someone in the neighborhood, and yes, pets. Leaving work colleagues behind can leave a vacuum in your life. For some, cutting this tie is easy and even desirable. For others, it is quite difficult, feeling no longer wanted by people who were once colleagues. The vacuum can be prevented with careful planning and the development of new relationships.

In the following, you will be analyzing your current relationships, how they will change, and what you would like to do about developing new ones. Think carefully about who your friends and close family are and which ones you expect to change with retirement. Talk with them and get their ideas and begin looking at how you will establish new relationships to replace the ones you will be leaving behind.

Assessing Changes in Your Relationships

Relationship Assessment Tool

List 5 People at Work That You Share or Shared Your Ideas and Feelings With on a Regular Basis	If You Are <u>NOT RETIRED</u> Check (√) Those People Who You Will Continue to See After You Retire	If You <u>ARE RETIRED</u> Check (√) Who You Continued to See After You Retired
1.	1.	1.
2.	2.	2.
3.	3.	3.
4.	4.	4.
5.	5.	5.

List the 5 Most Important People in Your Daily Life	List 5 People in the Community That You Consider to be Good Friends	List 2 Organizations or Religious Groups Where You Are Activity Involved or Want to Be Involved
1.	1.	1.
2.	2.	2.
3.	3.	
4.	4.	
5.	5.	

List Any Other Significant Others You Consider to be An Important Part of Your Life (professional colleagues, pets, etc.)	List 5 Spiritual Beliefs That Are Important To You	List 5 Things About Other People That You Value
1.	1.	1.
2.	2.	2.
3.	3.	3.
4.	4.	4.
5.	5.	5.

Examine your responses carefully. Think about changes that will make you feel like you have lost someone. Which of these friends and acquaintances will change with retirement? Who do you want to keep seeing? Is that possible and do they want to continue having contact with you? Now think about what your resources are going to be after retirement that will help you find new friends.

List 6 Places or Groups Where You Have Friends	Check (√) Those Which Will or Did Change With Retirement	Check Which Ones Are or Were the Most Important to You
1.		
2.		
3.		
4.		
5.		
6.		

How can you become more involved with people? How are you now involved that will increase the likelihood of making meaningful *new* relationships? In the following, list some specific things that you can do to establish new friends, new colleague, or new acquaintances - and - a time framework for doing this. For example: join the hospital auxiliary, participate in a theater production, attend cultural activities, be a volunteer, or take a philosophy course.

List 6 Sources to Contact	Give Your Primary Goal in Making Each Contact	Indicate the Deadline Date by Which You Will Make Each Contact
1.		
2.		
3.		
4.		
5.		
6.		

Take a few minutes to consider how changes in any of these relationships are affecting you right now. What changes do you see in the future and how might those changes affect you? What about friends and family members who are moving away? What about friends and family members who are much older? And don't forget about any pets in your life.

Remember, your dog is with you 24 hours a day. Your kids aren't. Guess who may know you better?

CHAPTER 5

YOUR "SELF"

Working and work related roles and responsibilities have a tremendous impact on your self-esteem or self-worth - sometimes positive, sometimes negative. In any job, as you get older, you are recognized as the most senior employee who has vast knowledge, experience, and wisdom. You get perks for a job well done. Others look to you for advice. You provide a service to your customers. You contribute to the goals of the organization, and you help younger employees learn the "*business*" and develop their own skills. You get inner satisfaction from knowing you have done something well, and that you are a senior spokesperson. You probably know more than others about what you are doing – or least you should by now. Your job gives you and your family an income, financial security, and many of the material things that you are important to you. It also gives you status in your family and sometimes even your community. As you retire, you are applauded for your contributions.

There can also be some detrimental things that can happen as you get older. Your knowledge may become out of date. Perhaps you don't produce enough and don't meet the expectations of the boss. You have to learn new skills to stay current and you have to learn to use all the latest technology. You may be out of touch with the younger employees. You don't applaud the hottest pop idol, and you don't understand what they call music. You put up with the criticisms, the stressors, the difficult employees and customers and you wonder why you are still working. You might begin to notice that your contributions no longer make you feel worthwhile and you no longer feel valued. These are clues that maybe it's time to retire!

Older workers are frequently replaced by younger ones with less experience, less knowledge but more education, less commitment to the organization – and frequently *more pay*. As a result, you feel like you are no longer important, and perhaps that you were not really valued in the first place. Think about how many times you have said, *"He's just a kid and he doesn't know half as much as I do."* And then he replaces you. Dwelling on who will – or did – replace you will not help you make it through the transition; in fact, it can make it even more difficult. So, he's a kid and he doesn't know as much as you do. Now it's his time to learn – just like you had to do when you started.

With retirement you will need to look for new ways to boost your self-esteem and make you feel good about yourself. Consider how you will use your time and what interests you. Think about how you can make a meaningful contribution to others. Playing golf three days a week may be a lot of fun, and you may get a lift in your spirits from shooting under par, but that is not the same as making a *meaningful* contribution with your life.

I Will is often more important than IQ.

Situation

> Hazel had been a college professor for many years and greatly enjoyed what she did. She related well with students, had a research program in nursing, and had many colleagues that had become close friends. Before she retired she began planning for what she would do and how she could replace all of those interactions with students and faculty. She thought about what she enjoyed and what skills she had. About two years before she retired, Hazel joined a book club and bought membership in a gym. After she retired, she continued to meet with the book club every Monday night. Three times a week she went to the gym. She joined a yoga class that she really

enjoyed. As a church elder, she became much more active in her church. On Saturday mornings, she read to children at the library and during two weeks in the summer she went to the Dominican Republic with her church to do physical exams on kids living in poverty. The transition to retirement for Hazel went very smoothly and she wondered why she had not retired sooner. She no longer had ties with her former colleagues, but had formed new friendships and new support groups. She had planned for retirement and her plan had worked!

Assessing Changes in How You Feel About Yourself

Start by looking at where you are, how you feel about yourself and how you believe you are going to feel after retirement. In the following table, identify those things in your work setting that made you feel good and list how you think they will change after retirement. For those that made you feel good, write down which ones you will miss. Rank them in order of importance and then discuss them with someone you trust and value. And be honest! You have absolutely nothing to lose and much to gain.

You got some of your inner *"warm fuzzies"* as a result of interactions with other people. Now consider the things you want to do after retirement. Will you do them by yourself? With other people? And remember, unless you decide to go back to work, you may be retired for many years to come, even decades. These days, some people are retired longer than they worked. As you make your list, consider whether you can continue what's on your list into later life. Are these temporary interests, or are they things that you will be of interest in 10 or 15 years? Are they active or sedentary activities? Will you *be able to do them* in 10 or 15 years? Do you want to work for pay? How flexible are your hours?

If you are alone, without a spouse or partner, perhaps you want to consider dating again. Use caution as you make your choices about who to date. Don't discuss your entire past and be careful about sharing personal information like finances. Try going out to dinner or meeting in a public place. Attend a concert, but decide in advance who will drive, who will pay, where you are going, and what time you will be returning home. Then, be careful who you invite into your home. Not everyone has appropriate intentions. Move slowly and think about what you like and don't like about the person you date. *Get references* from people you know and trust. What are the motives of the other person in wanting to date you? After saying all of that, having someone new to share your time with can be a rewarding experience and really add to your self-esteem.

Spend some time thinking about what makes you happy. Talk about your lists with other people. Then work on some strategies for making them happen. Here are some ideas to consider that *do not involve working for pay*. We'll talk about the "*work jobs*" later.

Activities to Consider

Coach kids on sports teams
Study Spanish and take a trip to Spain
Organize a fund-raising event for your local high school band
Take cooking lessons in a French country house
Develop an exhibition to display photos and paintings by kids
Work for a summer on a Native American reservation
Teach fly fishing on a camping trip to Boy Scouts
Help Boy Scouts get their Badges
http://www.scouting.org/scoutsource/BoyScouts/AdvancementandAwards/Merit Badges.aspx
Listen to Wagner's entire *Der Ring des Nibelungen - Das Rheingold* (*The Rhine Gold*); Die Walküre (The Valkyrie); Siegfried; and Götterdämmerung (Twilight of the Gods)
Become a receptionist at the information desk at your local hospital
Take up horseback riding
Organize a dinner club
Enroll in yoga class
Learn to swim
Take a course in landscape painting with water colors
Take up photography as a hobby
Go treasure hunting or search for gems
Go hiking in a national forest
Organize a bridge, poker or chess club

Self-Esteem or Self-Worth Assessment

List 10 Things That Make You Feel Good About Yourself That Do Not involve Your Job	Check (√) If You Do This Alone (Not With Other People)	Check (√) If This Can Be Continued In Your Later Life	Check (√) Those Which Will Change or Did Change With Retirement
1.	1.	1.	1.
2.	2.	2.	2.
3.	3.	3.	3.
4.	4.	4.	4.
5.	5.	5.	5.
6.	6.	6.	6.
7.	7.	7.	7.
8.	8.	8.	8.
9.	9.	9.	9.
10.	10	10	10.

As you consider leaving the work setting and moving into retirement, think about the things in your job that you really enjoy. What makes you feel good about yourself and what you are doing? Consider what you will miss the most, and surely you will miss some things. How can any of these things be replaced with other activities? Who else can you include in what you do? What do you want to do all by yourself?

List 6 Things That Make or Made You Feel Good About Yourself at Work	If NOT Retired, Check (√) Which Of These Will Be Missed	If Retired, Check (√) Which of These Is Missed Now
1.		
2.		
3.		
4.		
5.		
6.		

Now, list the things associated with work that you do not [or did not] like. What annoys you the most, gives you the most stress? What do you really want to leave behind? These may be the biggest reasons you are retiring, other than your age. How will your life be different when you no longer have these things to worry about or bug you? What are the advantages of no longer having these things in your life?

What about working bothers you the most?

1.

2.

3.

4.

5.

6.

7.

8.

9.

10.

Next, compare the two lists – what makes you feel good and what bugs you? Look at how they are different.

Think about 5 things that make you feel the BEST about yourself. Then, for each one, give one reason you believe it works for you. Perhaps it is spending time with family, raising your own vegetables, going hiking, or playing games with the grandkids.

Name the Activity	What About This Makes You Feel Good?
1.	1.
2.	2.
3.	3.
4.	4.
5.	5.

A Working Retirement

Many retirees really don't want to quit working completely. They retire from a long time job, but want to continue using their knowledge and skills. They want to continue to be a productive member of the work force. Perhaps it's due to needing extra income, but for many, it is just because they enjoy the kind of work they do. They enjoy being involved in their career, just not full-time. Or maybe they want to enter a new career, and try out a new type of job. For some, it is a way to continue being useful, productive and needed. It adds to their self-esteem. Whatever the reasons, there are a variety of things to consider. Ask yourself these questions:

Questions to Ask Yourself	Your Comments
What type of work do you want to do?	
Do you want full-time or part-time work?	
How many hours per week or per month do you want to work?	
How much travel time would work for you? How far from home could your new job be?	
Why do you want to continue working?	
What is the activity level you want? (physical and mental)	
What additional education or skills might you need?	
How much pay are you seeking? or do you want to volunteer only?	
What additional expenses would you incur?	
What impact would working for pay have on your Social Security and income taxes?	
When do you want time off?	
Do you want an Internet only job?	
Do you want to do only consulting?	
Do you have a current resumé?	
How do your family/friends feel about your continuing to work?	
How would working impact your home roles and responsibilities?	
Who do you contact about applying for a job?	

Now consider your responses and discuss them with the important people in your life so you can make informed decisions.

CHAPTER 6

SUPPORT WHEN THINGS GO WRONG

Having the support of other people when you need them, especially in times of crisis, is an important ingredient in surviving the inevitable difficulties of life. Crises can be relatively minor in one situation and seemingly unbearable in another. But, they are eased with the caring and understanding of family and friends. And you probably don't use the same support people for all situations. Family and friends will be there for you when you get sick, or when a tree falls on the driveway in an ice storm, or when the washing machine breaks down. Co-workers are there for you when the budget isn't balanced, the boss is in a bad mood, and production quotas haven't been met. Many times there is a carryover effect however, and co-workers are important in times of personal crises as well. Because you work closely together, they may very well be the people who bring you dinner when you're sick, move the tree off the driveway and make suggestions for a washer repairman. In *"small-town"* America, your boss, your co-workers, your family and the *"church goers"* may be all the same people. Yet in our extremely mobile society, having family close by is more and more unlikely. What happens to your support system if *you* move someplace else? Or if *they* move someplace else?

One of the most important things to understand is that support groups change considerably over time, and will continue to change after you retire. Prior to retirement, some of your support is provided by co-workers, supervisors, and friends associated with the job as well as from people outside the work setting. With retirement there is no longer the need for support for work related issues. Those issues, those problems, no longer exist. Co-workers retire, move away, and lose interest in remaining in contact. Over the course of your working years you probably had a number of different support groups. They may have changed with where you worked, where you lived, and even your own interests and circumstances.

> *Your presence may be more important than your words.*
> *Sometimes what a person needs is not a wise*
> *sage, but a gentle heart that listens.*

With retirement, the majority of your support will probably not come from people from your old job. Family members and friends move away. Perhaps you have also relocated. And one of the more distressful realities of aging is that older family members and friends die. For people in their 80s and 90s, it's not uncommon to hear, *"I am my own support system." "I don't have any family and all my friends are dead."* Developing support systems that can remain intact, ones that can change when needed, and developing new ones that are be available when you need them, are all important parts of moving through life. When you have friends and family who are young, middle aged and older you have greater stability.

Consider who you will have for support when you no longer work, when you can no longer drive, or when you are can't repair your house or clean up your home. What if you live alone, and you get sick? What if the person you are living with develops a serious illness and requires constant care? Where can you locate day care for an ailing parent or someone to visit a loved one in an assisted living facility? What if your vision gets bad enough that you can't drive your car? These are real issues. How are you preparing for them if, or when, they actually happen? The realities of aging need to be a part of your planning so you have support as you move along on your journey.

Assessing Your Support Systems

In the following table, list people or groups who you turn to in the time of need and for support when problems occur, whether minor or major. Then look at how these support systems will change with retirement. Then in the next table, list sources of support you think will be available to you after retirement. Who will you turn to, and for what type of support? Remember, think about later life, not just the next two or three years. Talk with your friends and family and see what they think. And think about how you will be a part of a support system for the significant other people in your life.

Support System Assessment Tool

List Your 5 Primary Support Systems or People that You Have for Daily Needs and Crises	Indicate for Which Problems You Look to These People for Support
1.	1.
2.	2.
3.	3.
4.	4.
5.	5.

Although support systems are not always immediately available when you need them, they can be called upon in times of crisis. In the following, list situations when you needed support. Then consider ways that you could go about developing additional support systems. Finding new support systems becomes an on-going process throughout life, including in later life when most people are more dependent on others for assistance.

There are a number of places to look. You may want to get to know your neighbors better. Check out any available newspapers and the Internet for health and financial resources, Find out what services are available in your community. There are local health care agencies, the health department, social services, and free tax services. There are excellent resources available on every topic imaginable on the Internet. Think about what would work for you and what is realistically available to you, as well as what you can financially afford. Locate free services, but always *look out for scams*.

List Major Situations In the Past 10 Years When You Needed Support	List Ways You Could Develop New Support Systems to Meet Your Needs
1.	1.
2.	2.
3.	3.
4.	4.
5.	5.

Next, consider what you will do in the next 10 years. Rethink the same issues concerning the need for support groups. Who do you have available to you now that will still be available to you in 10 years? Then consider what you may need support for in the future. Health care? Transportation? Cleaning your home or yard? Help to care for someone in your home? Financial support? Personal crises? Walking the dog?

List the Persons You Believe Will Be Available to You over the Next 10 Years When You Need Support	List What Types of Things You Believe You May Need Support for in the Next 10 Years
1.	1.
2.	2.
3.	3.
4.	4.
5.	5.

CHAPTER 7

CHANGES IN YOUR LIFE STRUCTURE

Think about this. Retirement is one of the few times since early infancy that you have nearly total control over your own life – how you spend your time, how much time you spend on what, when you get up, when you go to bed, what you do during the day and when you do it. When you were a child, your parents told you what to do – at least they tried! By the time you started to school, you met the requirements of the school. You got there by 8:30 in the morning, studied, had recess at 10:15 am, lunch at 12 noon. You did homework in the evenings, participated in scheduled sports or extracurricular activities, and played with your friends on the weekends. Much of your days were structured for you around your school activities and responsibilities.

If you went to college, you followed the time schedule of the college – the college's week, the college's semester and the college's year. You could pick some of the times for your classes, but the times were established by the college. You were off on Spring Break and holidays. Your work schedule was organized around your class schedule and you partied on the weekends.

As an adult, you had work schedules, PTA meetings to attend, children to take to soccer practice or dancing lessons. Your job determined which days you worked, when you had time off, when you took your vacation, and sometimes even what you did in the evenings and on weekends.

**We always want more time, but when we get it,
we don't always know what to do with it.**

When you retire, the structure you've had all of these years from your job *abruptly stops.* For the first time in your life you're the person in control of what you do, when you do it, for how long, with whom and how often. This is a totally new concept for retirees - and a baffling one for many. For some, the first year or two is so filled with events and activities that we frequently hear, *"I don't know how I had time to work." "I'm so busy I'll never get everything done." "Everybody wants me to do something for them. Now that I'm retired they figure I have all this extra time on my hands, but I don't. I'm already busy."*

For others, it's like walking in your front door with no calendar for the day, the week, the year, or the rest of your life. You don't have to set the alarm, which can be nice. You can go to bed when you want to, take a nap in the afternoon, go shopping, take a trip – and there are no constraints on when you do what. But that's exactly the point – there are no constraints – no structure. It's now up to you to provide the structure and as much as you want or need. Or, you can be a *"couch potato"*, but that won't be very interesting. It will get old along with you, and neither one of you will age gracefully.

No structure. No purpose. No life.

Understand also, that you may have other people and circumstances that create or even impost some structure for you as you retire. This can come from the people you live with, the organizations you belong to, or the commitments you have made. If you have a spouse who has a chronic illness and requires care, this can impose structure. If you have an elderly parent that you check on once a week, this can impose structure. Nevertheless, all of the time issues associated with work no longer exist, unless you go back to work or *"unretire"*, so to speak. Even then, you can control when, where, and if you work.

Putting some sense of structure back in your life is a part of the transition process and certainly a part of an effective adjustment to retirement. What do you want to do? When do you want to do it? With whom do you want to do it? What time will you get up and go to bed? These are new questions faced by the retiree. Some people handle it very effectively. Others don't. A total lack of structure can lead down the path to loneliness, feelings of uselessness, and certainly to inactivity. Think about how many times you have taken a two week vacation and at the end said, *"I'm ready to go back to work."* Of course, maybe you didn't! In retirement, you are on a vacation of sorts, but there is no work to return to when the two weeks are over. Try a *practice retirement*. Going cold turkey may not be in your best interest. After all, retirement is one of those things that you've never done *permanently* before. Take two weeks off from work. Don't go anywhere on vacation. Turn off the TV. Unplug the computer and don't do all those repairs to the house. After all, there's a limit to what needs to be done and you can't spend your entire retirement repairing the same house. Then ask yourself, *"What am I going to do with myself for two weeks?"* Don't do anything related to your job. Map out a schedule for two weeks. What's important to you right now? How will you structure your days? What will you do with your time? Who else will you include? What will you do alone and what will you do with someone else? And don't make this a time to do all the chores you have been putting off for a year. That defeats the purpose of the exercise. Think long range. Think about *"what if"* this is how I am going to live for the rest of my life, perhaps for the next 30 years or so. What am I going to do with myself? Then, go about doing it. What makes you happy? What do you like and what don't you like? What do you want to change? At the end of the two weeks, think about what you want to do to prepare for your *actual* retirement.

Assessing Changes in Your Life Structure

In the following, consider how your job structured your life and how retirement will change this. Add other things you do at the end of the list. Figure out how this could provide structure and meaning in your life.

Activities	When You Do Them Now	When You Will Do Them After You Retire
Go to a movie or concert		
Take a vacation		
Go grocery shopping		
Have the car worked on		
Visit family & friends		
Clean the house		
Mow the lawn		
Pay the bills		
Go out for dinner, movies, etc.		
Feed the dog, cat, etc.		
Empty the dishwasher		
Do the laundry		
Go to church, synagogue, temple		
Get up and go to bed		
Eat meals		

List 10 Ways in Which Your Job Provides/ed Structure to Your Life	Check (√) 10 Things That Will Change or Did Change With Retirement
1.	1.
2.	2.
3.	3.
4.	4.
5.	5.
6.	6.
7.	7.
8.	8.
9.	9.
10.	10.

Now, return to your *Weekly, Monthly* and *Yearly Calendars*. What do you want to change that will provide you with some structure? List your ideas and changes below. Make comments on the right side as you go along.

Changes for Developing Structure in Your Life

Changes You Want to Make in Your Calendar or Plans for After Retirement	Additional Comments and Ideas About Your Plans for After Retirement
1.	
2.	
3.	
4.	
5.	
6.	
7.	
8.	
9.	
10.	

CHAPTER 8

USE OF ALL THAT FREE TIME

Closely related to changes in the structure in your life are changes in the use of your time. Structure implies consistency, planning, and a pattern that you follow. It will vary from time to time and with circumstances, but there should still be some dependability, some stability in your days and weeks. Use of time focuses more on things you actually do with your time and the reasons that you are doing them.

Retirement lets you spend your time without spending your money.

We've already said that as an employed worker, much of your time was consumed by work and work-related activities. Your job determined when you got up in the morning, what days you had off, when you took your vacation, what you did for over 40 hours a week (and for some, much more than 40 hours). But it was more than that. You went to work and did what was expected. You talked with customers, did the budget, taught classes, prepared reports, kept appointments, and other work activities. With retirement, you now have the opportunity to spend your time primarily the way you want to, without the constraints and dictates of a job. You now have control over what you do and when you do it. You may have friends and family to consider, but that's very different from the mandates of a job. Think about how you have been spending your time. How much of your time was used for job related activities? With retirement, when work responsibilities are gone, how *will* you spend your time? How can you adjust to nothing but free time? Too many people wait until they retire to figure this out. *"I'll have plenty to do." "What am I going to do? I don't know, probably not much." "I'm going to enjoy doing nothing."* Well, *"nothing"* can be fun for a while, but *"all nothing"* gets very boring, very fast. And besides, it's not constructive. It doesn't contribute to the world around you, and doesn't make you feel like your life has meaning. Analyze your recreational use of time and then your meaningful use of time. Retirement is a new beginning and needs to be treated as a new adventure, rather than a time to do nothing.

Time is a drug. Too much of it kills you. Terry Pratchett

Plans for how you will use your time can also be interrupted by unpredictable situations and events. What happens if you can no longer drive, and you can't travel, or go out to dinner, or other things you had planned? What if finances don't allow you do the things you wanted to do after retirement? How are you going to handle these situations and how can you plan for them? Contingency plans are essential for a well-adjusted retirement. How would these things impact your life and the lives of those around you? How can you change what you do with your time?

Using time involves more than just planning things you like to do. For a balanced approach, you need to include things that you can do alone and things you can do with other people; things that are active and things that are inactive; things that are meaningful and things that are truly recreational, and things that exercise your mind as well as your body. You need things you can do with family and friends, time for the organizations you belong to, and time for the events you want to attend. And time alone. You don't have to be with your spouse or friends every minute of every day. Distance can sometimes be invigorating...!

By doing things alone, all by yourself, you have the time to reflect, be independent and do things that you personally enjoy. It puts some space between you and those around you, and it also put some space between them and you! Even couples who have been married for many years nearly always comment that they need time alone and away from one another. In fact with retirement, one of the problems that couples experience is that they have too much time together and need some space. When you were working, you and whoever you live with, spent 8-10 hours a day, or more, apart. That is 40-50 hours per week that you did not see each other. This assumes you did not work at the same place, of course. Now you have the potential of spending those 40-50 hours per week together. How do you plan to spend that time? Can you tolerate each other that much and for all that time? Can you live that close together in an RV or smaller apartment? For some couples, it's ideal because they enjoy each other's company. For others, it just doesn't work. You will need to figure out what is best for you, but don't take for granted that everything is going to go smoothly.

If you live in a retirement community, or a CCRC (Continuing Care Retirement Community), there will be more activities for you to be involved in that you want to do. There are committees, BBQs, afternoon teas, meals in the dining room, concerts to attend, bridge clubs, religious services, and social gatherings. You can chose what you want to do, and with whom you want to associate. There are exercise programs, and some even have indoor pools and recreational facilities. There may be a golf course nearby and tennis courts on the premises. You will be associating with many retirees and all have similar things in common. The age groups vary, but are usually people about 60 and older. It is common for the average age to be 85 and these people are healthy, active, energetic, and involved in what goes on around them. Retirement life is the now their focus with all the associated benefits.

More and more of the baby boomers, however are electing not to retire at age 65. While the data are changing, about 7 in 10 are planning to work after retirement, and 40% of people 55 and older are still working. Retirement age has become a moving target. Finances for older adults took a hit during the recession of 2007-2009 and this continues to impact their decision to keep working. Many of those who retired early did so because of one or more health problems.

Sources: http://www.gao.gov/products/GAO-12-172T; http://www.ml.com/publish/content/application/pdf/GWMOL/MLWM_Work-in-Retirement_2014.pdf

There are many activities that are cost effective and promote self-satisfaction. By using your time to pursue activities with friends and other family members you have the additional opportunity for socialization, for learning what's going on in their lives and their problems, as well as experiencing the stimulation of adult thinking and conversation. If you spend time with kids or grandkids, you get to enjoy the wonders of childhood again, and yes, even play with their games and toys! These outlets become a source of input that can make you feel good about yourself and allow you to make others feel good as well.

> *It is every man's obligation to put back into the world at least the equivalent of what he takes out of it. Albert Einstein:*

Both *active* and *inactive activities* are extremely important, especially as you age. By being active, including exercising, you are helping your body to remain healthy and energetic. By working with a health care provider such as a physician, nurse or exercise specialist (trainer), you can develop a routine that is best for you and that you can continue over time. Playing tennis, biking, jogging, walking, or working in the yard are just a few ideas. Many cities and even smaller communities are now addressing the concerns of older adults, their housing, transportation issues, and developing walking and bicycle paths. Having a planned weekly exercise program that you can do alone or with other people is important to your well-being and self-esteem. Having a partner to exercise with increases the likelihood that you will actually do it. Exercise also helps to keep your weight under control as you grow older! Remember, seniors who move to retirement communities usually gain weight…!!! Learn about nutrition and how to maintain a healthy body. Plan to be one of those folks in their 90s on treadmills and running marathons.

Did You Know?

In a study of men and women with MBA degree who graduated between 1973 and 1982, 20% indicated they wanted to work after the age of 65.

Source: Frieze, I., Olson, J., & Murrell, A. (2011). Working beyond 65: Predictors of late retirement for women and men MBAs. *Journal of Women & Aging, 23*(1), 40-57.

It is equally important to develop alternative activities that do not require you to be energetic and physically active. These are the things that you want to continue for a very long time and into later life. What are your hobbies? What new ones do you want to learn?

Did You Know?

Having a hobby can lead to a more positive retirement.

Source: Scherger, S., Nazroo, J., & Higgs, P. (2011). Leisure activities and retirement. Do structures of inequality change in old age? *Ageing & Society, 31*(1), 146-172.

You may like to paint ceramics, play the piano, make stained glass lamps, or make wooden bird decoys. Maybe you want to make toys, or doll clothes. These types of pursuits can be done alone or even with a group of people that you've invited for a special social gathering. But most importantly, they give you pleasure and suggest you don't have to be jogging down a wooded path every day to be active and happy.

There is the difference between doing things that are recreational and things that are meaningful. This doesn't say that things that are recreational cannot be meaningful, but there is a difference between the two. Doing something because it is recreational is for fun and you do it simply because it's fun. The reward comes from just doing it. This might be boating, fishing, growing flowers, or going to the movies. In contrast, doing something because it is *primarily meaningful* implies that the reason you are doing it is to contribute something to others as well as yourself. You are meeting the needs of someone else, or perhaps a group or even society in general. It makes you feel useful and important because it is a contribution. Activities in this category might include being a Red Cross Volunteer, a teen counselor, taking calls at a telethon, serving meals at a senior center, or helping veterans locate jobs. It could mean being involved in the committees in your retirement community. The point is, you need to be involved in activities that allow you to give something back to the people and the community around you, as well as doing things just for fun.

We commented on pets and their importance earlier. There is considerable research that suggests pets contribute very positively to everything from self-esteem to reducing blood pressure and decreasing the health risks. Having a pet is a personal choice and that is up to you. But walking the dog is not only exercise, it is constructive use of your time. Getting up to let the dog out puts you on a schedule – Sparky is not going to let you sleep in all morning. He needs to be fed, whether it's on your schedule or not. He wants to be played with, loved, and groomed. He needs to be taken to the vet. All of these become a meaningful use of your time, and a meaningful contribution to *"someone"* else. You get fulfillment out of taking care of your fuzzy friend and in return you receive a great many inner rewards – and unconditional love.

Time on The Internet

First of all, do you have a computer? If so, you can skip most of this section. If not, consider getting one, and keep reading. You can even get refurbished ones quite inexpensively. Go to your local computer store, there are many, and talk with one of the computer techs in the store. Have a price range in mind and have some idea of what you want to use the computer to do. Examples: email to family and friends, search the Internet for travel sites, make airline and hotel reservations, write letters (the old fashioned way), get a social media account, do your taxes, learn a foreign language, or take an online course. Ask the computer store salesperson for recommendations for a computer that will meet your needs and then make your decision. You can go to the local library and use their computer to look up computers on the Internet. The librarian can help with that if you've never used one before. There is a lot to know about computers and you won't know it all. You will want to have sufficient memory on it to do what you want to do, and these days, that is not a problem. Do you want a PC or personal computer that sits on your desk or do you want a laptop that you can carry around the house and take with you when you travel? You will need an Internet connection. Your local cable service can provide that – for a fee. You can bundle your cable, phone, and TV into one lump sum with many Internet providers, and even pay online. There are other resources where you can just go online and skip the other things, even watch TV and listen to music on the radio. You can also forget about the computer and get a tablet (sort of a mini computer) to do much of what you want. Again, talk with the salesperson about your options, or check out magazines on computers at the library. Some of those can be pretty complicated, though.

If you don't know how to use a computer, check with the local public library, senior centers, churches or temples, and the newspaper for short courses you can take on word processing (writing letters and other stuff), spreadsheets (for your taxes) and PowerPoint slides if you want to do presentations for your local civic group. Check to see what comes with your computer and what software you will have to purchase. That is extremely important because software can get very expensive. Then find somebody who can load the software for you, or learn how to do it yourself. There are many private stores that offer this service for a nominal fee and you don't have to pay big bucks at the big chain stores.

Once you have the computer, it's time to practice. Experiment. And always have a computer person at that local store you can call if you get stuck. Better yet, contact some of your family members and friends. There will undoubtedly be somebody in your circle that knows a lot about computers and can help you. These days, just ask any kid! They all know how to work these things. Then go back to the computer store and look for any software that you might want to purchase. You must have an anti-virus program to prevent unwanted and damaging intrusions into your computer. Next, learn which of your private information you want to protect and do not want to put on your computer. Learn about spam mail and phishing mail. These are emails that some unscrupulous character sends out to get you to buy something that doesn't exist, or send money to for an unworthy cause, or get you to sign up for something that you don't want. The basic rule is: If you don't know the person who sent it, delete it. Don't even open the email. Learn how to handle junk mail. There are a lot of books available that can walk you through anything you need to know and all of the information is readily available on the Internet with a quick search.

So what can you do with the computer beyond what was just mentioned? If you are planning a trip, get on the Internet and search where you are going and learn about it before you leave. You can find history, tourist attractions, hotels, restaurants (and make reservations online), transportation systems, and airport maps. For larger airports there are even virtual tours where you can actually see where you are going and how to get around in the airport. This is especially valuable in a foreign country if you don't read or speak the language. Remember, large airports can be very confusing for the novice, older adult traveler, or if you get lost easily. Some airports require a lot of walking, but many now have special shuttles, moving sidewalks, and trains. You can make all of your reservations online, and in fact it is frequently cheaper. There are sites that can compare your hotel rates, your airline rates, and get you a rental car. Check for any age limits and license requirements with the rental car company before you book, especially for foreign countries.

The Internet has a wide variety of resources you can access to get information. Take a French course if you are going to France. Learn about the Greek islands before you leave on a cruise. Learn new math skills and study astronomy. Get the latest local news and then search what is going on elsewhere in the world. Follow the stock market. Watch movies and listen to music. Watch sporting events and check team scores. Live videos are readily available where you can actually watch events as they are taking place. Be careful, though because some of these sites cost money.

Develop skills to chat with other people on the topics of your choice. After the initial investment, this is a phenomenal opportunity to be in touch with people at a very low cost (it's cheaper than phone bills), and learn about virtually any topic of interest to you - and some that are not. Don't be alarmed if you think you can't handle a computer. The basics are extremely easy and the skills can be learned quite rapidly. You can then advance as far as you want to. Ask one of the neighborhood kids to show you how!

There's one major problem, computers can become very addictive and the amount of software is incredible. You can travel the world while you sit at home, read about absolutely any subject, stay informed on current events, do your banking and pay your bills, find recipes, and even get a college degree. You can get a camera on your computer and connect to your children's or grandchildren's computers. You can actually see and talk with them. Most laptops now come with the camera already built in. You can talk in *"real time"* so that you can see them and they can see you You can both hear what one another is saying. That's a wonderful addition for families and friends who live long distances apart. Watch the grand baby learn to walk. Listen to your kids' problems. See the new car or new living room furniture you friend just bought. Use the usual cautions of being careful who you talk to and don't give out information you don't want other people to have or to know. And be careful what you post on social media because it's there for the world to see. Beware of posting those precious photos of you and the grandkids. Sexual predators also read those pages.

Time for Activities and Exercise

The words *"activities and exercise"* are used here to mean very different things. Activities are those things you engage in that you generally enjoy, that give you pleasure, and are of interest to you. Sometimes you even have to do activities that you don't like just because they need to be done – like take out the trash and clean the bathroom. They can be active or passive. They can be sedentary, like playing cards or doing a puzzle. You can do them alone or with other people. Exercise, however, is used to mean physical movement that energizes you, that becomes some degree of exertion for the purpose of training and extending the capability of your mind and body and physical fitness. Exercise is crucial for healthy living. There are so many choices available that it is literally up to you to choose what you want to do, what is best suited for you, and what meets your own health requirements. Get a physical exam – a check-up – first!!! You may have regular doctor visits. Or you may not have been to a physician in years – not smart!! Put that on your list of things to do in the very near future. Walking, membership in spa or gym, attending aerobic classes, swimming, Yoga, Tai Chi, and biking are some options. Buy an exercise bike and put it on the back porch or in the basement, even in the bedroom if that's the only place it will fit. The point is, *Do Something.* Avoid becoming addicted to the television or more recently to the Internet – which is unfortunately what many retirees do. Don't use the computer as a job substitute – or a therapist.

Television does not promote social interaction or longevity, unless of course, it's Sunday afternoon football with friends! And some grandmas and grandpas have had their e-mail addresses ultimately rejected as junk mail because their grandkids received so many that they got tired of reading them! A university professor, who already received tons of emails every day from students and other faculty, was getting about 50 emails a day from his aunt in a retirement home. She sent him everything from the latest news, to jokes, to recipes, to travel trips, to places she wanted to visit, to…you name it. Remember, just because you have time to send 50 e-mails a day doesn't mean the other guy has the time – or interest – to read them!!! This applies equally to texting.

You May Have a "Tech Addiction" if…
- Your laptop is the centerpiece on your kitchen counter.
- Your Facebook account keeps getting bigger.
- You spend hours every day *"gaming"*.
- You spend a lot of money on Internet site purchases.
- You lie about how much time you spend on your computer.
- Your kids know they can sleep from 1-5 am. You won't be texting.
- A free Internet connection is your first criteria for a hotel reservation.
- You send text messages to your spouse– in your own house.
- Your kids now refer to you as a "known user".

Exercise can promote not only physical health, but emotional well-being as well. After a physical check-up, develop an exercise program that is best suited for you and that you can continue in some fashion over the years to come. Because exercise is so closely related to health, consider how you rated your health on the assessment form and what you need to do to either to remain healthy or become more so. You might also visit the website of the American Heart Association for some additional ideas. http://www.heart.org/HEARTORG/

Keeping your weight under control is a part of the exercise program that you decide to follow. The 2010 Social Report says that roughly 36% of people 55-64 years of age and 33% of those 54-74 are obese (http://www.socialreport.msd.govt.nz/health/obesity.html). Unless you are, or want to be, a part of these statistics, keeping fit is essential. Obesity is well known to contribute to diabetes, hypertension, and cardiac diseases. As you age, you are already at risks for these, so why increase the risk by being overweight? Your metabolism slows as you age and fewer calories are burned up with your activities. Poor eating habits are the other factors that you can actually control. Just because you don't have parents to yell at you any more for all those desserts doesn't mean you are free to indulge in whatever you want. When retirees move to live in retirement centers, especially those with a food plan included, it's common for them to gain at least 10 pounds during the first year. And that weight is hard to lose. The temptations are there. The food is great. You don't have to cook and the menu gives you plenty of options. Restraint and exercise are key. If you go out to eat, all of the fast food restaurants have calorie counters for their food items online. Many of the big chain restaurants have the same thing and laws are changing that will require more of this information to be published in the menus, or at least available. *Read Before You Eat.* Check the calories online before you go to lunch or out to dinner. Figure out what you *don't want* before you get there and then get tempted to order every high calorie item on the menu.

But it's not just calories you need to watch for, its salt. Sodium causes fluid retention and has been linked significantly to hypertension (high blood pressure) and related to a number of other risks, like heart attacks and strokes. You only need less than a teaspoon (1 tsp salt = 5.5 g. = 2,132 mg. sodium) of salt a day to maintain a healthy balance of your electrolytes. The American Heart Association has recommended 1500 mg. a day maximum. Many Americans consume over 3000 mg a day. At some of the chain restaurants you will find that in an average meal of soup, salad with dressing and an entrée you can consume over 8000 mg in one meal. A fast food cheeseburger can contain over 700 mg. of sodium, and a double can have 1200 mg. or more. With fries an additional 350 mg. Processed and canned foods you find in grocery stores are notoriously high in salt. Get in the habit of reading the labels – before you buy, rather than when you get home and regret what you bought. Then, take the salt shaker off the table. Try cooking with a small amount of salt, especially on veggies. You will actually get used to tasting vegetables and meats like they really are. If your first taste is salt, then it's got too much.

Situation

> When my husband and I were first married, we went to his mom's house for dinner. She served the meatloaf and all the trimmings that the entire family praised and loved. The meatloaf was so salty I couldn't eat it. It felt like it was burning my mouth. On the way home, I made the early marriage mistake of criticizing my husband's mother's cooking. Well, learned from that one! Needless to say, an argument followed…one of our first, albeit not the last. I began to *de-salt* my husband's food. A year later we went to his mom's for the same dinner. *He* couldn't eat it. We have commented for years about those two dinners and the tremendous change that we made in his diet. He is now *de-salted* and has been for four decades. He enjoys the taste of green beans, and peas, and even meatloaf – without excessive salt. Salt should be used as a flavor enhancement, not as a condiment!!!

The next question to ask is, *"How is the health of the other important people in your family? Your spouse? Your children?"* Following retirement it is not unusual for one or both of you to develop serious medical problems. This sometimes just goes with getting older. But these problems can dampen your ability to be independent, as well as do the many of the things that you had planned to do. This is further complicated if you suddenly find that you're responsible for the care of an aging parent, or if one of your children moves in with you – along with two kids, a parakeet and a puppy. These situations pose their own set of challenges, but they certainly will affect how you spend your retired years. If you had planned a variety of activities, and new issues prohibit you from doing them, you will have to develop alternative plans - *if* you are to continue to live an enriched and healthy life.

When problems arise, and they do, having a support system is essential. You need people to talk to, to get suggestions, and actually help in the time of crisis. One of the things that retirees sometimes do, however, is decide when they retire that they are going to relocate – move. Think about how you answered that question on the questionnaire and consider the ramifications. When retirees move to a new location, especially immediately following retirement they are usually leaving behind friends and family members who were a part of their support systems. They may have been neighbors, relatives, members of their church or synagogue, people they knew through organizations, and so on. Finding replacements for these people can be difficult and take time. While you can connect by phone and e-mails with people you still know, it's not the same as having someone next door to call when you need something or just to take you shopping. Before you move, begin to develop ties in the new location, meet people, find organizations you want to belong to, clubs you plan to join. Do a thorough investigation of the community and find out if it will really meet your needs.

Before you move, consider who your friends will be. How will changing them impact how you live your life? What about medical facilities and medical care? What recreational and cultural resources will be available? Can you afford them? What's the climate and how will that affect you? If you're moving south, can you tolerate the summer heat? Can you afford the air conditioning bill? What types of transportation are available, especially if you find you cannot drive later in life? Once you move, develop local support systems and new friends. This doesn't mean you have to break relationships with the people in your previous friendship circle, but it does mean you need to begin to integrate yourself into a new one. No one can do this for you. Take the initiative and seek out other people, other resources, and other contacts. The decision to relocate needs to be carefully thought through – with all of the ramifications – *before* moving. Many retires have moved successfully and many others have regretted the decision.

Did You Know?

Residents in continuing care retirement communities (CCRCs) and even their children may not always be willing to share how they feel about their losses and grief associated with the move because the CCRC is viewed as a status symbol.

Source: Ayalon, L. & Green, V. (2012) Grief in the initial adjustment process to the continuing care retirement community, *Journal of Aging Studies, 26,* 394-400.

Situation:

Bill and Susan lived in upper Michigan and Bill retired from a small business where he was in charge of contracts with customers. His wife had been a school teacher. Bill's family was not originally from that area, but Susan was part of large family that lived there. They had two children in other parts of the country who were married and had children of their own. The day after retirement, Bill and Susan packed up everything and moved to Louisiana because it was warmer. Within six months Bill was depressed and they were spending a lot of time driving back and forth to Michigan to see her family. The climate was much more humid and hotter than expected. The home they bought was out in the country and not close to any neighbors or friends. After three years of this arrangement they decided to move again, not all the way to Michigan, but about half way in between, and near where one of their sons lived. Things improved considerably, but within a short period of time, the son and his family moved to the West coast. Once again, they were no longer near their family. They had clearly not planned well and had made some choices they continued to regret. They moved again.

An additional problem with relocation is you're not only moving away from family and friends, but you're also moving away from your primary health care providers – physicians, nurses, dentists, your accountant, the chiropractor, and even the veterinarian. Before relocating, ask for referrals and make appointments with them in advance. Transfer your medical, dental and veterinary records, including X-Rays before you move. With electronic medical records, this is quite easy to do. It is not in your best interest to wait until someone gets sick to make an appointment or to try to find a physician, dentist or vet. You need to develop a relationship with these professionals, establish trust and confidence, and they need to get to know you and your history. You need to know whether they accept Medicare and your type of health insurance. Not all do. Ask for suggestions from friends in the new community and ask for referrals. You can search physicians on the Internet and find out if the doctor you are considering has had any legal or ethical claims filed against him or her.

Time to "Senior-Proof" Your Home

Don't forget to *"senior-proof"* your home – *now* – so you don't have to later. If you have had kids or grandkids, you know about child proofing your home, but now you need to think about making changes that will *"senior-proof"* it. This can help to prevent falls, keep your medications in order, and make the daily chores of life easier for you. For example, throw rugs can be dangerous and cause you to slip and fall. The website of *Canadian Senior Years* has a number of great suggestions (http://www.senioryears.com/ageproofhome.html). Put railings on stairs in the house and outside. According to the CDC, each year 2.5 million older adults are treated in ERs from falls. Over 95% of hip fractures are caused by falls. Check out this site: http://www.cdc.gov/homeandrecreationalsafety/falls/adultfalls.html

Have lights placed so you can see what you are doing. Put things on lower shelves so you don't have to use a stepladder to reach anything. Put colored tape strips on the floor to show changes in elevation or if there is a stepdown. Put non-skid rugs in the bathroom. Install a grab bar and put a nonslip mat in the shower or bathtub. Keep clutter off of floors and keep electrical cords out of your walking path around the house. Routinely pick up the dog toys and put them in a safe place when not being used by Fido. Each week put your daily medications in a storage container labeled with the days of the week. These are cheap and readily available at pharmacies, and they can prevent taking too many or too few of your meds. Install a security alarm system and make certain your smoke and carbon monoxide detectors are working. Have everything checked January 1st of each year. Install a peep hole in the front door so you can see who is there *before* you open it. Cover up those lovely, trendy, but extremely dangerous hardwood floors. Many predict that the hardwood floor trend is going to reverse!!! They can be very slippery, especially when wet. Above all, have a working, charged, phone readily available in case of an emergency. Know the numbers to call. Put them into your phone. Carry your doctor's number with you when you leave the house, along with a list of all the medications you are taking. When you travel, keep your medications with you. If you found yourself in an emergency room for some reason, they are going to need that information quickly. *Never* pack your medications in your shipped luggage. I was actually on a plane when a woman across the aisle was having serious cardiac problems. Her medications were in the belly of the plane.

Time to Prevent Problems

Polypharmacy

Polypharmacy is a huge problem among older adults. It refers to taking many medication or drugs at the same time. In addition to prescribed medications, over the counter or OTC drugs and herbal supplements are frequently used. Taking these in addition to prescription drugs, and particularly without the knowledge of your physician can be not only risky, but very dangerous. Before taking any OTC preparation, consult with your doctor or nurse and find out what complications could result. When you get a check-up or when you travel, take a list of your prescriptions with you, but also include any OTCs that you are taking. Know your medications, why you are taking them, what they do, and when you are supposed to take them. Know the side effects. There is also frequently the temptation among older adults to try out new medications, new cures, and new OTC remedies. They frequently don't work, cost a lot of money, and they're not always regulated. Talk with your physician *before* you try them out. If they cure everything they claim to, why don't physicians prescribe them? Another temptation is to take the medications someone else is taking. While this is extremely common among the older population, it is also extremely dangerous. *Avoid the temptation.* Never, ever take anyone else's medications. First of all, if it was not prescribed for you, it is not your medication. These meds can have interaction effects, side effects, and even toxic effects with other medications you are currently taking.. And don't loan any of your meds to someone else.

I was staying with my aunt and uncle when finishing my doctorate. My uncle came home one evening for dinner and complained that his tongue was swollen, his hands were swollen and he was having trouble talking. When I inquired about any medication he was taking, I quickly learned that he had taken some meds that his friend at work was taking for his *"cold"* – the same symptoms my uncle had. I asked my uncle if he was allergic to anything? He said, yes, penicillin, but the bottle didn't say *"penicillin"*. I checked the bottle of the *"borrowed meds"* and it read Ampicillin…this *is* penicillin. I flushed the meds down the toilet, gave him some Benadryl and said *"Call your doctor"*. He recovered quickly, but this could have been disastrous if he would have had an anaphylactic reaction.

When the expiration date on your medication arrives, throw the med out or better yet, take it back to your physician or pharmacist so it can be disposed of properly. There is growing concern about pharmaceutical pollution when drugs are flushed down the toilet or poured in the sink. (Source: http://www.health.harvard.edu/newsletter_article/drugs-in-the-water). Talk to your local pharmacist before you flush drugs or toss drugs in the trash. There are rules to follow. There are an increasing number of community-based *"take-back"* programs that offer your safest disposal alternative (Source: http://www.fda.gov/ForConsumers/ConsumerUpdates/ucm101653.htm). The FDA's website provides further guidelines for the disposal of unused medications. Be aware, if you throw drugs in the trash, someone else may be there to take them back out again. I once saw a whole container of tranquilizers that had been thrown in a dumpster. Kids, pets and addicts could easily have helped themselves. The person who threw them out could be held liable.

Time to Prevent HIV AIDS

Most people probably don't associate HIV and AIDS with the older population; however, the National Institute on Aging reports that nearly 1/4th of the people with these diseases are age 50 and older. You can't get HIV/AIDS from public restrooms, shaking hands, and hugging a person with the disease, but you need to be aware and adhere to protected sex, and yes, even at your age. Source: https://www.aids.gov/hiv-aids-basics/hiv-aids-101/how-you-get-hiv-aids/

If you've ever injected drugs or had a blood transfusion in the 1970s and 80s, or if your spouse or partner did, you should get tested. Ask your doctor at your next check-up and be informed.

The reasons for the increase in HIV/AIDS among older adults are rather complex. Not all older people practice *"safe sex"* because they consider it something for the younger generation to do. They just don't think they can get it. Not true. Some older adults use illegal drugs and are even less knowledgeable about HIV than the young people of today. Some older adults may face discrimination issues when they consider getting tested or reporting any symptoms. And a lot of health care professionals don't consider the possibility of HIV/AIDS when they are doing assessments on older adults. Thus, be informed, talk with your doctor, nurse, or physician's assistant and protect yourself. If you have concerns, get tested. And condoms are readily available at any pharmacy, but they do no good if you don't use them.

In 2005, Persons Aged 50 and Older accounted for

- 15% of new HIV/AIDS diagnoses [1]*
- 24% of persons living with HIV/AIDS (increased from 17% in 2001) [1]*
- 19% of all AIDS diagnoses [1]
- 29% of persons living with AIDS [1]
- 35% of all deaths of persons with AIDS [1].
- The rates of HIV/AIDS among persons 50 and older were 12 times as high among blacks (51.7/100,000) and 5 times as high among Hispanics (21.4/100,000) compared with whites (4.2/100,000) [2].

Source: Centers for Disease Control and Prevention (CDC). http://www.cdc.gov/hiv/topics/over50/resources/factsheets/over50.htm

---

Time for Extra Income and "People Contact"

Many of the larger chain stores and fast food restaurants are hiring older workers for a variety of jobs. If that interests you, talk with the human resource people at the ones nearest where you live. There are also ads on the Internet for part-time workers in some of these stores. AARP has a site that discusses their Featured Employer's Program and gives many suggestions. If you want to work part-time, consider delivering flowers for a local florist, be a greeter at megamart, become the bagger at a super market, assist teachers at an elementary school, or a become a library desk clerk. These aren't high paying jobs, but they bring extra income, are not physically exhausting, and only involve part-time hours. Be aware of how much money you can make and how it will affect your income tax. Talk with your local social security office or your accountant about that. Do you want to get a job? Think about why you might want to work and why you might *not* want to. What type of work would you want to do?

You *Might Want* a Part-Time Job			You *Might NOT* Want a Part-Time Job		
Reason	Yes	No	Reason	Yes	No
Need Money			Finances Adequate		
Lonely			Socialize a Lot		
Get Out of House			Like Being Home		
Occupy Time			Already Busy		
Somebody Says To			Don't want to		
Need Stimulation			My Mind is Active		
Need Exercise			Have Exercise Program		

Time to Use Senior Discounts

Many of the restaurant food chains, grocery stores, movie theaters, recreational parks, and super stores offer discounts for people over a certain age. You may get 5% off on groceries on Wednesdays, a small drink for a discounted price at a fast food restaurant, and a reduced price on everything you buy with a special discount card. But many people may not realize that travel agencies, apartment complexes, veterinarians, telephone companies, cable providers, electric companies, banks as well as local businesses sometimes offer discounts as well. You may have to qualify or fill out a form, but that's about all. Many of the hotel chains give the option of a senior discount when you make your reservation. Also check out the possibilities for a reduction in room costs, including AAA or if you are a retired federal employee. Check your AARP status and use the card when you travel. Train travel in Europe frequently has rates for people over the age of 65. Caution: many times senior discount rates for hotels, trains and airlines are actually *higher* than the rates you can get from other options. Look at the pull down menus if you are booking online. The US park service offers a lifetime pass that gets you special rates at all of their sites. Remember to ask about a senior discount as you shop and as you travel. Keep your options open for trying a different motel or airline, and certainly for having flexible travel days. The day you leave and the day you return can dramatically change the amount you pay for airline and train tickets. Amtrak currently offers a discount on train travel for seniors. Check their website to get the specifics. Do an Internet search on Senior Discounts and you will find a variety of sites that offer suggestions. Here is one example:

http://activerain.com/blogsview/3413841/senior-citizen-discounts-you-have-to-ask-for

Time for Travel on a Budget

You may like to travel and go places you haven't been before and visit friends and family you haven't seen in a long time. Travel can be a wonderfully rewarding way to spend your newly freed up time, but it can also be expensive. As already mentioned, many of the hotel chains offer discounts to seniors and discounts for belonging the AAA or as a government retiree. The Internet is your best friend for searching the most reasonable places to stay. You can also get apps for your mobile phone that will provide you with the cost of gas at specific stations wherever you are.

Using Your Time to Drive – or NOT

Transportation is one of the greatest concerns in the daily lives of older, older adults. Many towns and certainly all of the rural areas don't have buses and don't have trains. Many rural areas don't even have taxi cabs. If you don't drive, and don't have a car or truck you are totally dependent on someone else to get you where you need to go. This is a serious problem in the US and one that is so frequently overlooked. Without access to reliable transportation the older person can't take the dog to the vet for shots, can't get prescriptions filled, can't get to the doctor for appointments, can't do the grocery shopping, can't do…can't do… many things. As people age, this becomes even more relevant and profound. For those who either do not own a vehicle or for whatever reason cannot drive a vehicle, resources are quite limited in many regions and towns. Most metropolitan areas have transit systems, but they don't always go where you want to go, and may not make family and friends particularly accessible. Keep this in mind if you decide to relocate.

If you *don't* drive, or if you *shouldn't* drive, find someone to drive you when you need to go somewhere. Talk with local organizations, religious groups, and community centers. Check with local governments. Many have transportation programs designed to assist older adults. There are cities that, for a nominal fee, have special transportation for senior citizens and disabled persons. These make getting around more practical.

Of course, then there is the very sensitive question that each person needs to ask: *"When do I quit driving?"* Along with that, *"When do I turn over my keys and sell the car?"* That topic is beyond the scope of this book, but AARP has some excellent tips for you to consider: Source: http://www.mayoclinic.com/health/alzheimers/HO00046

Questions to Ask Yourself About Driving

1. Have you almost crashed or had "close calls"?
2. Have you put dents and scrapes on the car?
3. Do you get lost easily, even in familiar places?
4. Do you have trouble seeing or following traffic signs?
5. Do you react slowly to unexpected situations?
6. Have other drivers honked or yelled at you?
7. Have you received a number of traffic tickets?
8. Do you see well at night?

If you notice one or more of these cautionary signs in yourself (or a loved one) you might want to register for a driver-refresher course. You may also want to talk with friends and family members about *their* driving. The "We Need to Talk" program, developed by The Hartford and the MIT AgeLab helps drivers and their loved ones recognize warning signs.

It helps families initiate productive and caring conversations with older adults about driving safety. It's also a good idea to talk to a doctor about concentration or memory problems, or other physical symptoms that can lessen driving ability. Source: http://www.aarp.org/home-garden/transportation/info-05-2010/Warning_Signs_Stopping.html

If you need glasses to drive, then wear them. If you need hearing devices, wear those too. Know your limitations. Remember to get your eyes and hearing checked regularly. Listen to the people around you. Are they saying you shouldn't drive? Could they be right? Should you avoid driving at night? Should you avoid busy expressways and city traffic? Are you taking medications that could interfere with your reaction time? Do you have arthritis or pain that could interfere with your ability to react quickly? Consider other options you have like sharing a ride with someone or taking public transportation. Many of the organized retirement communities provide transportation for residents to go shopping, to get to doctor's appointments, and for cultural events in the community.

Use of Time Assessment Tool

List 10 Things That You Like to Do With Your Time	Check (√) If You Do This Alone (Not With Other People)	Check (√) If This is Active or Takes No Physical Energy	Check (√) Those Which Will Change or Did Change With Retirement
1.	1.	1.	1.
2.	2.	2.	2.
3.	3.	3.	3.
4.	4.	4.	4.
5.	5.	5.	5.
6.	6.	6.	6.
7.	7.	7.	7.
8.	8.	8.	8.
9.	9.	9.	9.
10.	10	10.	10.

Use of Time Ideas

- Check the Internet. Many sites include a listing of the community resources that are available. Locate service organizations. Visit national and international organization websites as well.
- Read the local newspaper for a listing of the various activities that are going on during the week. These might include free lectures, plays, sports activities, continuing education courses, and special events. Most of this is also on the Internet.
- Contact Road Scholar for a listing of tours and where they will be going on. These are global and can be accessed on the Internet.
  http://seniortravel.about.com/od/tourgroups/p/Elderhostel.htm

- Check job listings in the newspaper and at the local Employment Security Commission for part-time work.
- Contact the local community college or university for a catalogue of courses. Find out how you can register as a non-degree student or audit some courses.
- Contact the local RSVP and AARP chapters for information and get on their mailing lists. Check out their websites.
- Try something new. Join a dance class. Try cake decorating. Organize a seniors only quiz show. Start a photo club. Learn to play a musical instrument.
- Put in a rose or herb garden and donate the flowers to a local skilled care center for older adults. Share the herbs with neighbors.
- Organize a Morning Walkers Club for your neighborhood or at the local shopping mall. Put together a monthly dinner club with the friends you make.
- Visit the local Family Y and enroll in their activities and exercise programs.
- Contact your church, synagogue, mosque, etc. and find out what types of volunteers they need.
- Buy a bicycle or get some exercise equipment and set up a routine schedule.
- Take up a new hobby such as photography, ceramics, painting, sculpture, painting doll houses, or whatever interests you.
- Then check out some new and unusual ideas. Source: http://www.seniorcitizenhousing.org/47-posts-of-fun-activities-for-the-elderly-who-are-young-at-heart/

Situation

Elizabeth was a senior citizen who worked two days a week, was active in her church and used a computer there to stay in touch with the membership. She played cards with a small group of friends every Friday night, did her grocery shopping on Saturday mornings, drove her own car and cleaned her own house. She even cut her own hair. A friend of hers suggested she get a computer so that she could be on the Internet and learn new things, experience cybertravel and chat with friends and relatives via e-mail. She said, *"No thanks. I don't want one and I don't need one."* A few months later, another friend offered Elizabeth her laptop because she was getting a new one. Elizabeth reluctantly said she would take it. Her friend hooked her up to the Internet and increased the font size. A few days later Elizabeth was online and visiting a few sites, though still not totally convinced she needed a laptop! Elizabeth, by the way, was 91 years old. She lived to be 99 years and 10 months!

CHAPTER 9

PUTTING IT ALL TOGETHER — AFTER YOU "RE-TIRE"

By this time you should have a pretty good understanding of the six major areas where you are going to have changes. You know there will be changes in your roles in your family and life, your relationships with others, sources of feeling good about yourself, your support groups, how your life will need to be re-structured and how you might use your time. You have had the opportunity to consider what all of these changes could mean for you. Now let's get a better understanding of how these all fit together.

First of all, when there are changes in any one of these six areas, there are changes in the other ones. When something happens to one member of a family or a circle of close friends, it usually impacts the other members. When you change one piece of the system, changes occur in all of the other areas. Let's say you one member of a married couple. Mom catches a bad cold and can't do her usual chores around the house. Dad now has to do those chores in addition to his own. Dad doesn't have time to go to his meeting with his guy group tonight because he's fixing dinner. Somebody has to walk the dog and feed the cats. Then there's the laundry. Mom can't get to her hair appointment. The kids still need someone to drive them to soccer practice. Changes continue to occur until the cold goes away and stabilization returns to the family. This is a normal part of any family's life. When there is a major change for one member of the family, many other changes follow as a result. When there is a change in one part of the system, there are changes in the other parts. Now, let's look for a moment at what happens after you retire and how these various life changes influence one another.

Your Roles

Think about the role changes that occur when you go from being *employed* to being *not employed*. And remember, "*not employed*" is not the same as "*unemployed*". The latter implies a need or desire to be working. Changes in who you are, in your identity, impact directly on a number of things. They change your relationships – those at work, those at home, those in the community. They change the people you associate with, even the people that you know. You may or may not see the people you worked with any more. And if you do, you probably won't discuss the same things that you did when you worked together. In your role as a retiree, you may have new friends, new colleagues, and even associate with family members you haven't seen in a while. The people you worked with may also be retired and this sets up new kinds of relationships. Maybe now you play golf together, go shopping together or go on vacation together. This is an entirely different relationship than the one you had as employees. You may have moved and are trying to develop new friends, or you may already have them.

Your role as a retiree has changed how you think of yourself. You're not an employee or a boss, you're now a retiree. It has changed how you use your time, what you do in a given day or week, and what you plan for your future. Being a retiree has changed how you structure your days and the weeks ahead. You are hopefully looking at your support groups and looking for new sources of support. Perhaps you still have some of the same ones or had before, but you now use them for things that are no longer related to your job.

Your Relationships

The changes in your relationships in turn influence your roles. Maybe you have made a new friend and have some new roles. You don't see the people you worked with, but now you have friends in the organizations you belong to. Perhaps you have gotten to know your neighbors better, or you have moved and have new neighbors. Your relationship with your husband or wife may have changed and what you do around the house is different. Maybe you and your wife (or husband) have switched some roles. She got a part-time job and you are the one who now stays home most of the time. You help clean the house and do laundry, or have dinner ready in the evening when she comes home. Maybe you're living in a retirement community and go to the main dining room together for dinner. You and your wife have more time together and more time to talk, enjoy your hobbies or interests, and plan for the years to come. If you have taken a part time job, perhaps your wife is now doing more of the yard work. This changes your relationship with one another. If you're living in a community where the yard work is done by maintenance crews, and there is a housekeeper to clean the apartment, you have additional free time you devote to the things you enjoy most.

Changes in your relationships can impact your self-esteem, especially if you do not particularly enjoy some of the new roles you have developed or if you and the people you now live with do not get along very well. Maybe you don't have anything much to do and get bored easily. People around you will feel this too. New relationships can create new support groups. If you have to rely on other people for assistance, and yet don't really want to, relationships can become strained. The amount of time you spend with others is important and provides for both meaningful relationships and for some of the needed structure in your life.

Your Self-Esteem

How do you feel about being a retiree? This is important because how you feel about yourself can influence how you use your time and even what friends you want to be around. If you're feeling down or depressed, the odds are, you are not going to be using your time as effectively and productively as you could. You also are less likely to pick friends that are going to be enjoyable or who will enjoy *your* company. In fact, you could be lonely and feel isolated. You may be delighted with your new role in retirement and thoroughly enjoying it. You feel really good about where you are in life. By changing who you see and what you do with your time, you can directly impact how you feel about yourself. Getting some structure into your life can provide you with a sense of purpose and direction. Continue looking for constructive things to do with your time and interesting people to see. Watch for local events that interest you. Consider your travel plans and how they could impact how you feel and what you enjoy.

Did You Know?

It's estimated that 40% of older adults feel lonely.

Source: Bekhet, A. & Zauszniewski, J. (2012). Mental health of elders in retirement communities: Is loneliness a key factor? *Archives of Psychiatric Nursing, 26*(3), 214-224.

Your Support Groups

Assuming you had some sort of support groups at work, for work related and even personal problems, you have most likely made some changes. You don't need support for work problems, but you do need support for some of what goes on in your life. You have learned that support groups change. People move away or you may have moved, and as you get older your family and friends will unfortunately pass away. The important lesson here is to constantly be adding new people that you can count on for support – if you get sick, if someone dies, if you can't get to the grocery store or need a ride to go to the mall. Your support groups are the basis for some of your relationships. Not only do you need support from others but they need support from you as well. This places you in the role of being a part of their support system while contributing to your own self-esteem. It can make you feel useful and valued when someone calls you for support, whether for a minor issue or a major crisis.

Your Life Structure

Not only does the structure in your life change, but retirement changes the lives of people around you. Remember, you are not going to work in the morning. This changes your habits and it affects the habits of others. It can create serious problems in relationships. If you are married, continue to talk about how much time you are spending together and plan for times that you can both be alone or with other people. There have been many divorces after retirement when two people who have married for years find that they don't know each other, don't like each other, or no longer have anything in common. The kids are grown and may have moved away. Your interactions with them have changed, and so has the focus of your conversations. Your job is no longer the topic of many of your conversations. Things you used to talk about may no longer have meaning. This is a time to develop new interests and new relationships. Most of all – talk about it and be willing to listen to what others are saying to you. Put some structure in your life that involves other people, but allow yourself to have some of your own space.

Your Use of Time

When all you have is *free time* it's important to develop and maintain constructive outlets. You may have so many things to do that you can't keep up with them. This is not unusual, certainly in the first year of retirement, if not for a few years. Remember to continue to plan a variety of activities including those that you can continue into later life – active and inactive, alone and with others, meaningful and recreational. Choose activities that stimulate your thinking, your reasoning ability, promote physical ability, that use your emotional sense, and the wisdom you have accumulated over the years. Yes, by now, you certainly have wisdom and others can profit from it.

Example

Jeff had been a philosophy professor. He was quite competent in Ancient Greek and Latin. He was an active writer and had written dozens of articles for journals and several books on philosophy. When he retired, he decided that he wanted to retain some of these activities. He began to plan his schedule, had some works in progress, and made contacts with publishers - before he even came close to retirement. After retirement he continued to write and to read everything of interest to him. His daily routine included one hour of doing math problems, one hour of reading, and one hour of writing. When he died at the age of 96, he was as sharp as when he first retired.

CHAPTER 10

THE PERIODIC "SELF-CHECK"

Personal growth doesn't start and stop on a given schedule. There is continual change. Adjusting to retirement and to the happenings and feelings of later life require an on-going assessment, a re-evaluation of all the changes in your goals, plans and strategies. In order to keep up with your progress and challenges, do a periodic self-check to revisit where you are and where you are going. In the following table, insert the specific dates you will do a "Self-Check" on how you are adjusting to retirement and to life in general. Save it in a convenient place. Then every few months take some time to re-examine where you are. Periodically, *"Hit Your Now What? Button"*…and make changes that will help you *Enter the New Retirement Age*.

"Self-Check" Table of Dates

Date	"Self-Check" Done	"Self-Check" Not Done
1.		
2.		
3.		
4.		
5.		
6.		
7.		
8.		
9.		
10.		

"Self-Check" – How Satisfied Are You with Your Life?

	Strongly Agree	Somewhat Agree	Sometimes Agree & Sometimes Don't	Some Changes Needed	A Lot of Changes Needed	Strategies I want to Try for Changes
I Enjoy the Roles & Responsibilities That I Have						
My Relationships With Others are Rewarding						
I Feel Good About Myself						
I have Support When I Need It						
I Have a Schedule of Things to Do						
I Enjoy What I Do With My Time						

"Re-Tire"

Enjoy The New Retirement Age

Retirement can be the greatest time of your life. Look at where you are now and where you want to be. If you are currently working, give some serious consideration to what is going to change for you and the people around you when you retire. If you are already retired, consider what changes you have already made, and make others that will help you with your journey. Practice communicating effectively with other people. You will avoid a lot of arguments and a lot of stress. Retirement means developing new things to do, new people to associate with, and a fresh new look on life.

APPENDICES

Understanding Some Facts

Recommended Daily Salt Intake

590 mg. of Sodium in ¼ tsp.

Maximum Daily Amount: 1 tsp. (2360 mg.)

Recommended Older Adult Daily Requirement: 1500 mg.

Source: Food Facts. US Food and Drug Administration (July, 2012). Sodium in Your Diet: Using the Nutrition Facts Label to Reduce Your Intake. http://www.fda.gov/Food/ResourcesForYou/Consumers/ucm315393.htm

Recommended Daily Fat Intake

9 Calories/Gm. of Fat

2000 Calories Per Day Needed

30% Maximum Calories From Fat = 600 Fat Calories

600 Calories Divided by 9 Calories/Grams equals - 66.66 Grams of Fat Per Day Maximum

Food Component	Percent Daily Value for 2000 Calories
Total Fat	65 grams (g)
Saturated Fat	20 g
Cholesterol	300 milligrams (mg)
Sodium	2,400 mg
Potassium	3,500 mg

Total Carbohydrate	300 g
Dietary Fiber	25 g
Protein	50 g

Source, Including Additional Food Components: http://www.fda.gov/Food/GuidanceComplianceRegulatoryInformation/GuidanceDocuments/FoodLabelingNutrition/FoodLabelingGuide/ucm064928.htm

Sodium Guidelines for Food Purchases

Salt/Sodium-Free   Less than 5 mg of sodium per serving

Very Low Sodium   35 mg of sodium or less per serving

Low Sodium   140 mg of sodium or less per serving

Reduced Sodium   At least 25% less sodium than in the original product

Light in Sodium or Lightly Salted   At least 50% less sodium than the regular product

No-Salt-Added or Unsalted   No salt is added during processing, but not necessarily sodium-free. Check the Nutrition Facts Label to be sure!

Source:http://www.fda.gov/Food/GuidanceComplianceRegulatoryInformation/GuidanceDocuments/FoodLabelingNutrition/FoodLabelingGuide/ucm064928.htm

Strategies for Stress Reduction

- Talk with a member of your clergy or another religious leader
- Develop an exercise routine [in consultation with your primary health care provider]
- Practice relaxation exercises
- Practice meditation
- Find quiet Times to be Alone
- Find times to spend with other people you like
- Participate in social activities
- Listen to music
- Take a walk
- Develop an activity program [exercise, biking, walking swimming, etc.]
- Enroll in a yoga class
- Work on time management
- Take an anger management course
- Consider marital or individual counseling
- Take a conflict management class
- Get a therapeutic massage
- Adopt a pet from a shelter

Suggested Internet Sites for Additional Information

Health and Exercise
Fitness Library
http://www.primusweb.com
Information on fitness and list of resources and books
The Calorie Control Council
http://www.caloriecontrol.org
Provides information on healthy weights, cutting calories and fat from diets
The American Dietetic Association
http://www.eatright.org/
Facts and nutritional resources

Fast Food Facts and Information
Fast Food Facts – Food Finder
http://fastfoodnutrition.org/
Chowbaby.com
http://chowbaby.com
Fast food information by fast food restaurants and type of food. Includes information on restaurants by location of city or town.
Calories Burned and Calorie Calculations
http://www.healthstatus.com/calculate/cbc
United States Food & Drug Administration
http://www.fda.gov/Drugs/default.htm
Information on food, nutrition, drugs and consumer services.
Weight Loss
http://weightloss.about.com/
Information on various weight loss programs.

Travel and Recreation
Sample of Reduced Cost Travel Web Sites
http://www.cheaptickets.com
http://www.expedia.com
http://www.orbitz.com
http://partners.priceline.com

http://www.travelocity.com/
http://www.traveltidingsusa.com/
http://www.trivago.com/

Travel Associations and Resources
American Automobile Association
http://www.aaa.com
RV Clubs
http://www.rv-clubs.us/rv-clubs.html
Go Camping America Directory
http://www.gocampingamerica.com/
Go RVing
http://gorving.com/where-to-go

Society of Government Travel Professionals
http://www.government-travel.org/assoclist.html
Information and links to variety of travel associations and resources
Travel Industry Association of America
https://www.ustravel.org/
Travel Clubs, Campground Associations & Organizations
http://www.kiz.com/campnet/html/cluborgs.htm
American Society of Travel Agents
http://asta.org/
Senior Citizen Travel
http://seniorcitizen.travel/

Samples of Volunteer Opportunities

AARP Senior Community Service Employment Program	http://www.aarp.org
American Cancer Society	http://www.cancer.org
American Lung Association	http://www.lung.org/
American Red Cross	http://www.redcross.org/
Boy Scouts of America	http://www.scouting.org/
Easter Seals	http://easter-seals.org
Girl Scouts of the USA	http://www.girlscouts.org/
The Humane Society of the USA	http://www.humanesociety.org/
Idealist	http://www.idealist.org/
International Volunteer Programs Association	http://volunteerinternational.org/
National Voluntary Organizations Active in Disaster	http://www.nvoad.org/
SCORE (Service Corps of Retired Executives)	https://www.score.org/
Senior Corps	http://www.seniorcorps.org/joining/rsvp/
The American Society for the Prevention of Cruelty to Animals	http://www.aspca.org/
United We Serve	http://www.serve.gov/
Volunteer.gov. America's Natural and Cultural Resources Volunteer Portal	https://www.volunteer.gov/gov/new/about.cfm
Volunteer Match	http://www.volunteermatch.org/
The Y	http://www.ymca.net/

Additional Volunteer Opportunities

Hospital Volunteer Programs
Library Reading Programs
Local School Volunteer Programs
Meals on Wheels Programs
Police and Fire Associations
Senior Citizen Councils
Social Organizations
Civil Rights Groups
Nursing Home Assistance Groups
Habitat for Humanity
Local & County Government Agencies
Local Cultural Societies & Organizations

ADDITIONAL RESOURCES

Taylor, P. On Retirement. 25 Things to Do When You Retire. U.S. News & World Report, February 11, 2011.

Senior Discounts-Find the Gold in Golden Years. http://seniordiscounts.com/

National Association of Senior Citizens® (NASC®). http://www.trademarkia. com/nasc-national-association-of-senior-citizens-78068783.html

The United States Social Security Administration. http://www.ssa.gov/

Centers for Disease Control and Prevention. Healthy Aging. http://www. cdc.gov/aging/index.html

HomeHealthMedical.com. Polypharmacy and Older Adults. Posted January 30, 2012. http://blog.homehealthmedical.com/2012/01/ polypharmacy-and-older-adults/

Modified Food Pyramid for Older Adults© (2007).Tufts University. Friedman School of Nutrition Science and Policy at Tufts University. http://nutrition.tufts.edu/research/modified-mypyramid-older-adults

About.com. Senior Living. Travel Smart. http://seniorliving.about.com/ od/travelsmart/Travel_Smart.htm